FITRA JOURNAL:
MUSLIM HOMESCHOOLING

First Edition, 2017

Copyright 2017 Fitra Journal
www.fitrajournal.com
Editor: Brooke Benoit

Design by Reyhana Ismail
www.reyoflightdesign.com

All rights reserved. No part of this publication may be reproduced in any language, stored in any retrieval system or transmitted in any form or by any means - electronic, mechanical, photocopying, recording or otherwise - without the express permission of the copyright owner.

CONTENTS

Editorial: Brooke Benoit 4

CHAPTER 1: BEGINNINGS 7
Why My Mum Homeschools Us: Iqra Arfeen 8
My Extended Educational Journey: Angeliqua Rahhali 10
Ask The Homeschoolers: Angeliqua Rahhali and Brooke Benoit 14

CHAPTER 2: THEORY, METHOD, AND STYLE 21
Interview with A Homeschool Graduate: Zawjah Ali 22
Three Teenagers, Three Approaches: Brooke Benoit 25
Unpacking This Unschooling Idea: Zakiya Mahomed-Kalla 27
Charlotte Mason Method: Respecting Children's Unique Nature: Dr Gemma Elizabeth 30
Avoiding The Pitfalls of Part-Time Homeschooling: Asma Ali 33
Memory Tips and Tricks for Effective Learning: Zawjah Ali 37
How to Train Your Dragonfruit: 10 Reasons to Cook with Your Kids: Klaudia Khan 40

CHAPTER 3: ORGANIZING AND RETHINKING THINGS 42
Whose Identity is it Anyway? Khalida Haque 43
Overcoming Self-Doubt and Second-Guessing: Umm Yusuf Aisha Lbhalla 46
Can You Be A Minimalist And Homeschool? Brooke Benoit 49

CHAPTER 4: OUR FAVOURITE RESOURCES 52
Bullet Journaling with Kids: Karrie Chariton 53
Typingclub.com is Mom Approved: Karrie Chariton 56
Best Children's Cookbooks For Hands On Educational Fun: Klaudia Khan 57

Our Contributors 60

Editorial: Have Less Worry and Find More Faith

By Brooke Benoit

I recently had a chat with some friends about anxiety in older people. Apparently, it's not uncommon for anxiousness and worries to increase as people get older. This is contradictory to what I had hoped for in my own deen. I thought that as I got older I would be more patient, more firmly reliant and faithful in Allah's (subhanallah wa ta'ala) will. One acquaintance explained that her elderly relative even worries about worrying, if he's worry about the right things, worrying too much or too little. Being an innate overthinking, of course that worried me! But then again, being aware of a problem is half the problem, right?

As you read the stories of homeschoolers, such as Angeliqua Rahhali's in this issue, you may be surprised to hear parents admit that homeschooling has been such a blessing and life changer for *them*. We parents actually get so much out of homeschooling, it can sound and even feel a bit selfish at times. Letting go has been a huge takeaway for me from my family's homeschooling experience. Not to say that I don't worry, but with seven children, I simply don't have enough hours in the day to worry like I did with one or two. Also, our homeschooling lifestyle hasn't panned out the ways I had hoped it would, but it persists and it works.

Having one child complete their highschool education has been a major relief for me. This is not to say that I am done with him, but it feels good to see that the process is working. I have worried a lot about this child, the stubborn one who rejected my initial homeschooling style choices and forced me to think further and further outside the box. Actually, he recently corrected me, "You didn't *homeschool* me, you *unschooled* me," which I am also thankful that he finally recognizes that distinction even if he still doesn't agree with the style! Therein lies another lesson I have learned through homeschooling.

I had expected my children to be thankful that I homeschool them. Having never been to school, well, they don't understand what they are missing. Sometimes they are thankful, and sometimes they are resentful. I have seen plenty of other families who regret having sent their kids to school, and their children are unhappy about it as well. While I remain flexible, willing to enroll my children in school if they want to, so far this scenario has never worked out. Ultimately I understand that there are going to be aspects of my parenting style that they won't appreciate or like, but that would happen whether I sent them to school or not. I can't please all of my children all of the time, and I simply don't worry about it anymore, instead I remain firm in doing what is best for all of us.

Homeschooling can produce a lot of anxiety, especially since it's still so radically different from what most of our contemporaries are doing. I don't fully know how to avoid that anxiety, other than continuing to pray about your choices and surrounding yourself with information and supportive people. I hope that *Fitra Journal* continues to offer you a balanced, full view of the possibilities available through homeschooling. It's so different for each family and even each child, take what you like, what works, and leave the rest behind. Find peace in knowing that there are others who have treaded similar paths and that while there is a lot of relief available at the end of the road, you should probably worry a lot less along the way.

Brooke Benoit, Founding Editor of *Fitra Journal* | editor@fitrajournal.com

Chapter 1
BEGINNINGS

Why My Mum Homeschools Us

By Iqra Arfeen

I wanted to interview my mum, Umm A'teeq, as I felt that her advice could benefit people who wanted to begin or are homeschooling. I was intrigued to find out why my mum wanted to homeschool. What made her do it? And I had many other questions... I thought it would be a great idea to help others through the answers my mum would give. I am the eldest, seventeen years old, and have just finished my GCSE's via homeschooling. So here is the interview and I hope you all enjoy and benefit from it.

Iqra: What made you want to homeschool?
Umm A'teeq: Alhumdulilah, I have six children: five girls and one boy. My eldest four had been through the schooling system from nursery, until three years ago when I pulled them out. The reason in choosing to homeschool my children was mainly due to my second eldest daughter in primary school getting bullied, which carried on to her secondary school years as the same girls joined her at her new school. The same thing then happened to my third daughter in same primary school, sadly the school was unable to deal with the situation in an appropriate manner as there wasn't a no-bullying policy in the school. This led us, as parents, to decide that the school was failing to provide security, which safety was one of the reasons we had chosen this school. At the same time I took my fourth daughter out of school too because I didn't want the same thing happening to her. Meanwhile, my eldest was at a secondary girls' Islamic school and was suffering from another issue: peer pressure. Her grades were going down as the crucial exam period approached, which was not good at all. She was caught in a downwards spiral and the effects were visible. This made me and my husband decide to pull our eldest daughter out of her last year of secondary school, just months away from her exams.

But my concern was not about exams or school at that moment, I was only focused on saving my daughter from the ill effects of society. So following the Sunnah of the Prophet ﷺ, I did my istakharah and pulled my daughter out. I was not worried about what would I do or how would I cope, I just put my complete trust in Allah ﷻ and had faith that He would aid me in this situation, and so He did. From there my homeschooling journey began, and I haven't looked back since, alhumdulillah.

Iqra: Have you faced any obstacles while homeschooling? If so, how did you overcome them?
Umm A'teeq: So far I haven't faced anything, alhumdulillah. There is a lot of support for homeschooling parents where I live. There are many forums, email groups, and websites

which constantly post advice and help for various situations. There are group gatherings every other week which were set up by a few sisters for children and has now grown and is still continuing to grow. There are trips, workshops, and activities carried out. SubhanAllah doors were rapidly opening up for me and I was enjoying the benefits of homeschooling.

Iqra: Was it easy to join in with the homeschooling community?
Yes. alhumdulilah, it was very easy to join the homeschooling community. They have been running for more than ten years and are very organised and welcoming to anyone who is homeschooling! Everyone is very friendly and we all share ideas and experiences while our children play happily at regular meet-ups. We all help each other to construct new trips and workshops for our children. Allah states in the Quran: "Whosoever puts his trust in Allah, He will suffice him." I truly understood this ayah as I placed my trust in Allah fully and He indeed was sufficient for me.

Iqra: What resources do you like to use the most?
Umm A'teeq: Google! (Laughs). I generally type in whatever I need and see what results come up. I do have some go-to websites which are:
1. https://imanshomeschool.wordpress.com/
2. https://raisingsahabas.wordpress.com/
3. http://www.sarahmuslimhomeschooling.co.uk/404546149
4. http://www.aweclub.co.uk/
5. http://www.amuslimhomeschool.com/?m=1

For curriculum based studies I used https://wolseyhalloxford.org.uk/ and http://www.oxfordhomeschooling.co.uk. These websites start from the beginning of high school and provided a lot of support and advice for my daughter through her exams.

Iqra: What advice would you give to potential homeschooling parents and beginners?
Umm A'teeq: My advice would be to make every experience in life a learning opportunity. Lessons don't have to be set and structured like school, the beauty of homeschooling is to be different and constantly be thinking of new ways to teach. For example one day your maths lesson could be while you're baking; measuring, cutting and timing are all to do with maths.

Iqra: JazakAllah to my mum, who has always been a great inspiration and guide for me and my siblings, for helping in writing this article and for allowing me to interview her. I hope everyone has benefited from this interview in one way or another.

My Extended Educational Journey

By Angeliqua Rahhali

I have always referred to myself in the digital world as a lover of learning. In the early years this was frowned upon and I found myself secluded from many for my wanting to get lost in a library and not hang out at the local mall. I was not alone and had the encouragement from my family and elders in our religious community that encouraged me to always seek knowledge and not rely on others to answer your questions. In teaching our children at home I hope to instill those same values and hungers for knowledge. In this article I will touch on a few aspects that have either been important to my family or have helped us to get to where we are today. A lot of time, effort, trust, and faith have gone a long way to helping us find peace of mind in our learning choices and educational path.

Knowledge at our fingertips

We will always be learning something new in our life whether it be a new hobby, a life skill (such as how to change brake pads), to possibly learning a whole new career. We live in a time where knowledge is so easily accessible with online research or even simple Youtube videos that visually demonstrate how to do something. I love that while homeschooling our children we have the freedom to fail and it hurts less with so much access. We have the freedom to get up and try again. The freedom to totally throw something out the window that might be causing frustration, and to start over. There is no one way to learn or just one style that will always work. Being able to be flexible and willing to face our fears has helped me to blossom as well as my children. My family has always made having access to the internet a priority and it is a key tool to aid us in teaching. Now with so many apps available on portable devices there really is no excuse for not being able to find information or to fact check while out in the world exploring. There are just so many methods to access information and no reason to leave questions unanswered.

Aspects of my educational journey

I would like to offer a little information about me that will help you understand how I landed on this path and why I have no label for the type of schooling that we do. I come from a brick and mortar public education but have one very important factor that guided me toward homeschooling. My family moved around and as we went from new school to new school I had to adapt to different teaching methodologies and regional learning styles. I even studied abroad to compare how schools in Europe were guiding their children to future successes. Schools in the Northwest area of the US and schools in the Southern parts have a basic core understanding when teaching children. However they differ drastically on where they place importance in education. Do you focus on tests and academics or do you go with a more open style and focus on extracurricular activities and arts? I was blessed to see the beauty of both worlds and had my eyes opened to the beautiful cultures and educational practices around the world.

My husband grew up in Morocco in their public school system and then went on to a private pre-outlined study track that does not give students the freedom to chose their own future. He only experienced the one path until he left home and came to the United States to see for himself how our schools approached teaching. From the limited resources and little choice in his path, he had a harder time being satisfied in the working world because it had nothing to do with what he loved or even liked learning about. As adults, he and I have had the joy of exploring our own interests outside of school and learning new hobbies that intrigue and stimulate our minds. We both felt we would be able to guide our children better and help them find their own paths of studying while they get a feel for the world around them.

Should learning be limited by age?

I am in no way a public school basher, if that works for your family then go for it. I know that it is always there as a backup for my family if for whatever reason I am unable to continue on the path we have chosen. Coming from that background I saw many good aspects that outweighed the negative. I however did not want my children being taught that the only way to learn is to pass a test and if you didn't pass then you were a failure. I wanted my children to fall in love with learning, to know that no question was a bad question and that they could study anything they wanted as they find new passions in life. Having been a teenager when my parents were taking college classes, and encouraged to attend with them, I found that gaining knowledge does not have an age or grade limitation. Yes some advanced skills need steps to be learned in a certain order, but you shouldn't be held back from trying to learn those new skills because of age limitations. I loved being respected for my ability to keep up conversations about historical figures with adults in classrooms that were not filled with students dreading opening a book. From this experience, I wanted to pass on this love of learning to my children.

The current point on our homeschooling path

The stage we are in now is a mix of middle school and high school topics as my children are trying to complete a good foundation of their basic skills before moving on to the next stage. We have been focusing on mastery of each subject without going backwards for further review if it can be avoided. Having made it this far, knowing that college and other journeys are right around the corner, I feel as if we have been homeschooling for a lifetime. There have been many bumps in the road and moments of self doubt as well as some deep soul searching to see if this was truly the path we needed to remain on. I know that Allah subhanahu wa ta'ala has guided our family on this journey for a reason and I have to keep faith that He will continue to put us where we need to be. We have mastered the early stages of learning and milestones of growth. Now, as we are in the stages of independent exploration and research, there are moments when we find ourselves dealing with internal battles that most teenagers face regardless of where they are going to school or how they are educating themselves.

Can you really teach your own children?
This is a question that I am faced with all the time in a world that is unfamiliar with homeschooling. After years of observing parents and adults around me I grew to understand that anyone can be a teacher because we are all teachers. We may not have a piece of paper on the wall with a title but that doesn't mean we cannot teach someone something. How many times have you had to help a child tie their shoes or brush their teeth? Did you need a degree for this? Obviously not. You may have needed to research methods to help with potty training and bedwetting issues or how to solve ongoing temper tantrums, but you did it and did not have to formally pass a test to do so. With this in mind I knew without a doubt I could teach my children.

I love researching anything and that is the first thing a pregnant mother tends to do. Research, question, and scrutinize every aspect of pregnancy to the early years of child rearing. When doing this research I started researching learning styles, early school methods and standards that I was expected to live up to based on societal norms of growth and education. During this research I came across endless amounts of curriculum, learning styles, activity sheets and a plethora of advice from well meaning veterans in the homeschooling world. I knew I was not the first to walk this path and I did not intend to reinvent the wheel. I know I will not be able to teach my children every aspect they need as they grow, but I can show them and guide them to the right tools that will help them. I can provide them with good surroundings that will help them to learn and grow in confidence.

Highlights of curriculum that has worked for us
From the very early stages of growth and development we used games and toys to demonstrate skills the kids would need to go on to the next step in life. With these games and toys we found that as they grew older and the activities became harder they still attached fun and playful ways to learning. We started our homeschooling in an unschooled way without grades or tests, just advancing on to the next level when and as needed. As the kids got older I wanted a little more structure but still wanted to give them the freedom to explore and discover. They studied based on their interests while making sure they did not fall too far behind in the basic tenets of children's education.

We explored different styles of learning from online-based resources to workbooks to even local classes and co-ops. In doing this we found that part of the year they liked to have a more structured internet-based study plan and other parts of the year they preferred to break away from that and use workbooks. Our workbooks have been varied and can be found online or at local school supply stores as well as thrift stores. Before putting money into a full system that might not get used or only tried for a month and then set aside, I like to explore the material and see what works for each child's learning abilities. One online program that has worked for us and we tend to go back to off and on, has been Time4Learning which is a supplementary educational website. I really like the method they use to teach and then quiz as you go along without too much stress. You can advance at your own pace and see the progress. The program also allows you to go back to previous levels in order to practice skills that you may be rusty on. To add to this program we use Netflix videos and documentaries, field trips to local museums and shops, as well as library books and other online resources.

As my children are growing older and their learning needs are changing we allow them to explore more thematic studies they are interested in. Along this path we still turn back to our beginnings of games and fun for learning, always trying to find something that can be added to their studies to make them more interesting and memorable. Now that they are avid readers we can have deep discussions of literature and compare books to movies and dramatic representations. We can take field trips to Universities and sit in on workshops with other peers so they can discuss topics of interests with them.

And the journey continues!

I have not pinned down one school of thought or full curriculum that works for us, instead we mix a variety of tools and studies to achieve an overall view of the world around us. When you go off to college you experience teachers with different teaching approaches, just as when you go into the workforce and have coworkers from many walks of life, experiences and age ranges. Trying to close off learning to just an age or class range is not realistic and I find that approach to be more of a hindrance than a help. We are taking school one semester at a time and allowing for breaks as need be. One subject leads to several questions which opens up more doors to explore and get lost behind. The path ahead of us is unknown but that is part of the excitement of lifelong learning.

Ask The Homeschoolers

Please submit your homeschool-related questions to editor@fitrajournal and we will have experienced homeschoolers answer them for you in the next issue.

Question: How do mothers interested in homeschooling convince their husbands?

Advice: I thought it would be interesting to see what my husband's take on this would be now. He swears he had to convince me to homeschool. This was not what happened, but he is welcome to think that all he wants. I know I was the one to bring this idea up having known homeschoolers in my lifetime and seeing their successes. This concept was foreign to him from the start. I remember when we first started talking about this we were both so new to the needs and wants of children. We were young and full of so many ideas about what we wanted differently for our children. We really had no idea what it would be like as many new parents are in the beginning. There was so much excitement, anxiety, stress and many dreams all starting up at the same time. I think every new couple faces some part of this or another. This is the beginning of forming a marriage and a family. There are always ideals versus reality.

I had my husband talk to other men about what their kids were facing in school and what they thought of the idea of learning at home. I wanted him to find out what experiences other people in his culture had been through with their own children. I wanted to see what his expectations were and to find out what he thought was realistic as far as education would be. At work he would ask anyone he came into contact with if they had kids and what they thought of their education, their schools, and so on. He was asking everyone about their experiences with schools and about teaching and learning in general. People from every walk of life, every corner of the globe. The majority of people would tell him that if they could they would homeschool. As more people supported this the more he was convinced it was a viable option. He would come home a few times each week with more and more excitement that homeschooling is what we wanted to do. As time went on and events in the media would portray what was happening in schools he would be reassured in our choice to teach at home.

Just like when you venture into something new you talk to your friends, your mom, whoever you feel most confident in seeking advice from. Your husband will need to do this as well. You will see that he will have questions from other men that you both are trying to answer. The most common being "How do they get into college?" along with queries about standardized testing. Everyone wants to know how you will prove they are ready to move on, how you will compare them with other students in the same grade. Have your research done for your state or country, and be ready to show him how that can be done when the time comes. Have him do some research of his own, point him in the direction of learning styles and needs. I have heard other women have had success by having their husbands meet up or talk with other homeschooling dads. That has been a big help in the line of convincing. They can see what has worked and what has not worked for other families.

As the years have gone by and our children have started voicing their personal views on their studies, we have had to readjust what we are teaching. We are always adjusting and reevaluating what areas are more important. If the both of you are from areas in the world that really put a big emphasis on grades and tests, then that is something he is going to need to see proof of. If social activities have more weight in his mind then that is something that he is going to need to be involved in. Both parents need to be included in the decision process and you both have to respect each other when making this decision. You may have to be willing to give a bit more and plan a bit more in order to really get him on your side. Be open to his suggestions and ideas as you want him to be to your own. He may have some hard points that you are not ready to face but his perspective and concerns come from the same place of love for your children and thinking of their future as yours do. As our children have gotten older we have had moments of doubt and concern about whether we really were doing what was best for them. We would take a break, rethink what we were doing, and try a new approach.

Our family is a bit laid back and dad is hands-on in areas I am not the strongest. Every so often he wants to see proof of what they are learning and how. He gives input that helps us to adjust our schooling accordingly. After that he goes quieter for a bit but is always supportive. We have found what has worked for us through many hours of trying new directions, successes, and some not so successful attempts. All of this has helped us to learn more about how our kids learn and see the world around them. Communication is so important at every new milestone. Find things that your husband is stronger at and have him work with the kids in those areas. One example for us is that he is very good with electronics and computers whereas I am not. So I have had him teach the kids tech stuff or come up with new projects to work on together. He has always loved chemistry and this has given him an outlet to learn and experiment in. He gets excited about learning something new that he never got to do in school, then he wants to show them everything, and in turn they get excited about it as well. Hope this helps.

Answered by Angeliqua Rahhali

Question: How to keep level-headed through it all????

Advice: The best advice I can give in this area, that may have helped me to know when I started on this path, would be to not feel like you have to do everything on your own. So many times I tried to reinvent the wheel, thinking I was doing what was best for my children when really I was hurting myself. There is so much information out there that sometimes you really have to be willing to let things go. You cannot control every aspect of learning and you cannot be an expert in every field or subject of learning. I myself do not have a background in childhood education or teaching, but I have spent many hours researching and hunting for information on each new subject we come across. It is ok to not know what to do, that is part of the fun of teaching yourself new subjects while you are teaching your children. There are so many families that have tread the path for us that I love learning what worked for others and what didn't work. This really helps to know that I am not alone and nothing I am facing is new (we quickly forget in the heat of a vicious meltdown that this is not the first child to face this problem.) As unique as I may think my situation is, I always find someone who has been there, done that.

In the beginning years we homeschoolers try so hard to find balance and do this schooling "right," that we easily face burnout and exhaustion. Look to those around you with the same mindset. Find a good support system so that when you need a break you have someone to help out or bounce ideas off of. We found park days to be the best outlet. No curriculum needed, just some snacks and toys, and let them go wild. I would drive around town when my kids were little and find playgrounds that had other kids and mothers using them. The kids would make new friends and I would chat with the other moms when I felt comfortable. By getting out of my comfort zone it helped me to not stress about what was left at home and really just enjoy the day for what it was. Sometimes we would take our activities and sit in the grass as well. Make a quick picnic and study under a tree or near a stream and just naturally let learning happen.

Another important point is to try and not lose sense of who you are as a woman, mother, wife, daughter, and so on. With all the hats we wear adding "teacher" and "facilitator" can be very daunting. You give up some of yourself in this process. Take time to reconnect with who you are and what you want your children to learn from you. Connect with your own spirituality and what makes you happy. Lead through example. This is like when people give new moms advice about sleep when the baby sleeps. Read when the kids are reading, paint or color alongside them. Sometimes you will just have to let that mountain of laundry wait so you can build with the blocks or hide out in a blanket fort. Little hands are always going to want to help in the kitchen or be nosy about what you are doing and it can get overwhelming. Give them a place that is safe to watch you and to ask questions. Give them little tasks like washing the veggies or counting things out. As they get older and their skills increase you can then have them plan with you. The kitchen is a whole world of learning unto itself. Try and see the world from their view and remember that more than not you are new to this too. You were a kid many years ago so you might need a little reminding of what they are going through.

Allow yourself to grow and change in the process of learning and teaching. You will discover in all the years of your own schooling there is a whole world of learning out there that you never knew about. If we as adults did not learn everything about every subject when we were young then give yourself a little slack and remember they will fill in the gaps as they go. They will grasp knowledge and suck it in at warp speed and be ready for more while you are still trying to wrap up the lesson from the day before. You may have to scrap complete areas of learning at times in order to keep up with their current hobbies. It's ok. Keep reminding yourself that each day is a new day to start over. Don't waste your precious bouts of energy trying to prove to all of those around you that what you are doing is the best for your kid, you do not need to validate your choices with everyone. Spend that time being the best you can be and really putting faith in Allah as he guides you through this process.

Answered by Angeliqua Rahhali

Question: Regarding all things high school and college, what is needed (credit hours/courses) to graduate high school? What testing is required to graduate from high school? The ease or difficulty a homeschooler may face applying for college. How to enter college early? What testing is required to enter college? What is needed credit /courses to enter college?

I'm not sure geographically where this question came from, but maybe that's good so I can try to answer it in a way that helps as many people as possible. The best advice that I received on this issue was to look at the end result and work backwards. So, look at the exact university or other end goal your child has in mind and find out what their entrance requirements are. The scary part of this is that children don't generally know for several years into their education what direction they want to go. And even though the homeschool child prodigies who go to uni in their early teens are the stories we will be most familiar with from the media, in reality homeschoolers can be late bloomers who fully utilize their homeschooling opportunity to explore themselves and their identities in their teens. They may not know their direction until later than you hope for. You may have to sit on your hands, as they say, for several years not having any sort of vision of how this will pan out.

In the meantime, especially if you are outside the US or UK, you will be told that it's impossible to go to university without a high school diploma, baccalaureate or whatever your nation's equivalent is. This is simply not true. It may be more difficult, but not impossible! Here in Morocco I have been told that repeatedly, so I did my research. The universities here are very competitive to get into because the state schools are all free. Turns out that for a homeschooler to apply, they will have to sit the same state exams as everyone else and follow the same application process of entrance exams, but can be accepted without having gone through the local high school process. These allowances were put into place so as to not exclude children who were unable to attend physical schools for whatever reasons. None of my children currently have an interest in attending university here, please read the article "Three Teenagers, Three Approaches" in this issue which explains what processes my family is currently working on with US colleges in mind.

In the US and UK I have known families, myself included, whose high school-aged children were able to attend community college or state college either concurrently while still enrolled in high school or just enrolled in university students through testing processes. Another thing to keep in mind is that it is the high school coursework, especially the last two years, that will be most relevant to college application processes, so I would advise parents not to stress about this issue for your child's entire education. Many parents feel more comfortable being enrolled in an accredited program for their children's entire homeschool education, though this isn't necessary unless you have plans to return them to a physical school. When you get close to the high school age, which it sounds like this reader is, be realistic about what is available to you locally or financially. Research the most likely options by reading their admissions policies and making visits to their office if possible or phone interviews to seek clarity on the process. You may need to enroll in an accredited high school program to receive a diploma, a baccalaureate, or a (fairly new) international baccalaureate.

Maybe you need to build a portfolio and/or take the GED. I have heard that some high school-aged homeschoolers just study for the SAT. Take comfort in knowing that statistically the majority of homeschooled children do go on to higher education, you've just got to take on the role of guidance counsellor and do the extra leg work to figure out how.
Answered by Brooke Benoit

Question: What if my in-laws don't want me to homeschool?

I would request my knowledgeable and veteran homeschooling sisters to help, guide, give advice, suggest to me as to what I should do. In my quest for understanding the homeschooling journey, so far I was alone by the will of Allah and have been gathering all information all by myself. Where I'm from, I have never heard of anyone homeschooling their children. It's completely a new thing. In spite of all this I have been trying to work out my decision whether I can homeschool or not. I have been informing my spouse and he too supports me 50-50%. I also have been praying and asking Allah ﷻ to guide me. I also prayed Salat al Istikharah twice in this month. So now my dilemma is after the Salat.

I have faced quite a few tricky and difficult situations regarding my decision to homeschool or not. To those of you who may not know, in our Asian culture the in-laws play a crucial role in all major decisions, whether or not the husband or wife approve of it. I am in this situation. My in-laws are quite dominant and try to create difficult situations for me. Even though my spouse says he supports me, eventually he gives in to what his family tries to convince him to do.

I ask you, sisters, how I should interpret the guidance from Allah? I am unable to decide whether to homeschool or not. Do the negative situations that I face mean anything?

I am residing in UAE and currently my in-laws have come to visit us. My sister-in-law lives close by and is also quite involved in most decisions that my husband and I make. If I homeschool they will continue to question my capabilities, they will use tactics to prove that I am doing something wrong and am ruining my children's educational future. I have already started to see their tactics as my mother-in-law was questioning me about how I'll teach them at home and my husband too was accusing me of purchasing homeschooling books and resources, saying that I am just wasting money and the children are not learning anything. The kids are 7.5, 5 and 2 years old and [it is occurring] in front of them, but I'm not sure they are understanding anything.

I want to start homeschooling with my daughter who is 5 years old this September. She will be going to Kg2, but is already reading at home with me whereas that would do the same in school only by the end of the Kg2. But because my husband's sister's son, who is just 2 months older than my daughter, got a Certificate of Merit my in-laws think I am just a fool. 'Why didn't my daughter receive a certificate if she was so smart?'
*This question has been modified for clarity.

Dear Sister,
As salaamu alaykum.

Thank you sharing your dilemma with us.

The decision to homeschool or not is your's and your husband's. In the process of this response I will not be telling you what to do as I do not believe that I know what is best for you and your children. You (and they) are the expert in that field. However, what I will try to do is examine your questions and attempt to provide you with explanations for your situation as well as explore ways in which you might deal with the concerns and negative feelings of the in-laws towards homeschooling so that you might be better placed to make a decision.

Your main enquiry seems to be around making the decision of whether to homeschool or not. Just to make things a tad more difficult I would like to add that there is a third option: you can do both. My understanding of salatul istikharah is that once you have prayed it you are meant to follow through by doing what necessitates the choice you are inclined towards: for example, if you want to homeschool you will start doing the things necessary to provide that or if you are unsure of what to do you seek the counsel of someone you trust in the matter. Istikharah is a derivative of the word khair and it means "to seek goodness or a guiding to righteous deeds and actions from Allah ﷻ."

From your correspondence it appears that following your isthikarah you are struggling to understand what it is that you are meant to do. On the one hand you can see the benefits of homeschooling your children and it is something you very much want to do. On the other hand the people around you seem to be against the idea. We hold on to our viewpoint, too tightly sometimes, because we believe that we are right. My belief is that life is not about being right but about doing right. Your dealings and interactions with Asian culturally attuned in-laws are conflicting with your wish to homeschool. A technique I often recommend to separate out the noise from the knowledge and understanding is to still our minds and to open up our hearts. Following an ordinary prayer or another istikharah or when you have some quiet time available to you: sit in a comfortable position ensuring that the soles of your feet are flat on the floor … this is to ground you … Then focus on your breathing and bring it to a slow calming pace … Allowing each in breath to provide you with clarity and each out breath to release confusion … once you feel you are at a steady pace and feeling still turn your mind to your heart and what you know … there *insha'Allah* (God-willing) lies your answer.

Often we know the right thing to do but fear or a lack of courage holds us back: what if we are wrong? What if they are proven right? Everyone is scared, whether they admit to it or not. Sometimes we cannot get rid of those scary feelings and so may have to take those feelings with us and do the very thing that frightens us. Once it is done we feel better – whether it went badly or well. The thing to keep in mind is: *Alhamdulillah* (All praise and thanks belong to God) in all circumstances but what can I learn from the experience?

Asian cultural practices can feel interfering. Particularly in regards to marital relationships and raising children. Firstly, it is important to recognize that people will do what people are used to doing. They don't necessarily mean ill. Secondly to keep in mind that if you and your husband can come to the same page on all (or most) matters then dealing with the views of others (be it your family/friends or his) will be easier. Thirdly that ultimately everyone is thinking of the children and hold the believe that their stance is what is best. And finally Allah ﷻ knows best and He is the best of planners. So if the children go to school or are homeschooled or indeed both … it is what is right for them. Actually even if children go to school it is essential that as parents we continue being teachers to them. Sending them to school does not mean we have no say or input into their learning. If they are at school, we need to keep a dialogue going with our children about what they are learning and experiencing there. For the same reason we need to develop good communication and relationships with teachers and schools.

I don't believe that I have answered your question, certainly not – perhaps – in the way you might have wished. We often want others to just make the choice for us because it feels so hard to make the decision. I think that we can only give advice based on our knowledge and experience and so the advice we give to others only really suits us, if we were in that situation … because we will be lacking some key facet that the person seeking the advice has. Through your handling of these difficult relationships in your life you will bi'idhnillah be modelling for your children how to behave with others.

I pray that my response has been of some value and that Allah ﷻ guides you to the best for yourself and your children in terms of Deen, Dunya and Akhirah.

Wasalaams
Your Sister in Faith
Khalida

Answered by Khalida Haque

Chapter 2
THEORY, METHOD, AND STYLE

Interview with A Homeschool Graduate

By Zawjah Ali

You likely know that the word "homeschooling" brings a lot of doubt and questions to most minds, and is not widely accepted. Imagine how difficult it would have been back in the days when the term was even less common. It took an especially fierce woman just over a decade ago to stand against the tides, to set an example of determination and courage. As it is quoted, 'A woman who walks in purpose does not have to chase people and opportunities. Her light causes people and opportunities to pursue her.'

Areeba Zubair, daughter of Umm Osama, is the answer to such critical questions raised concerning the social skills and education of homeschooled kids. She is aged twenty-two, mother of a baby girl, and intends to follow her mother's footsteps in homeschooling her own children, in sha Allah. Areeba is currently enrolled in a bachelor's degree program of Islamic Studies from an online university. I interviewed Areeba, the homeschool graduate, to inspire contemporary homeschoolers with her experiences.

Zawjah Ali: Are your husband and in-laws supportive of homeschooling?
Areeba Zubair: Initially, they were not very supportive of this idea. They were always coming up with some objection or another. But after the first few months of my baby's birth, my mother-in-law declared that Husna would be homeschooled just like her mother. My husband has announced it too. Alhumdulillah!

Zawjah Ali: Will you follow the same curriculum your mother used for you?
Areeba Zubair: Yes, I would follow my mother's method and curriculum because I am really satisfied with it. I would like to add and utilize all the resources that are available to us now, for which my mother had to sometimes compromise on and at other times to find alternatives.

Zawjah Ali: What was your routine during your homeschooling years?
Areeba Zubair: Fajr salah was accompanied by Hifz E Quran lessons. Then we would take a nap. We would study one subject after breakfast. Quran class/hadith/tafseer/tajweed was after thuhr prayer. This was a small class conducted at our place where neighbourhood kids and friends joined us. Two hours in the evenings were usually spent at Karachi Gymkhana for sports and library use. Quran revision was after maghrib. Book reading after isha and then sleeping. Arts and crafts, skills, and computer class were on the weekends.

Zawjah Ali: How many siblings are you?
Areeba Zubair: Seven: five girls and two boys.

Zawjah Ali: What is your mother's teaching style?
Areeba Zubair: She is an effective and inspirational teacher. She took any curriculum (usually we followed Oxford) and Islamized the concepts. She turned the kitchen into a science lab, we explored plants in the garden, and visiting historical sites and similar outings were part of the practical side of academics.

Zawjah Ali: Why did she opt to homeschool you?
Areeba Zubair: It started when we first moved to the UK in 2005, when I was in fourth grade. Her main focus was our Islamic upbringing and she was unwilling to compromise on that. Against a lot of resistance from my close family in the UK, she stayed firm and decided to keep us at home. She did not like the education system which restricted us and limited thinking and imagination to certain ages.

Zawjah Ali: What problems did you face during this time?
Areeba Zubair: A lot of criticism and resistance from uncles and aunts. They wanted to persuade my parents to send us to school. They feared that we would be inadequate in terms of technology and might not be able to cope with this era. Sometimes our routine would be very unstable especially since we travelled a lot.

Zawjah Ali: Homeschooling is relatively easy in initial years, how did she cope with your higher studies?
Areeba Zubair: She hired expert tutors, and would enroll us in revision classes almost four months before O & A level exams where we would practice past papers and so on. I took my GCSE (O level Equivalent) from London as a private candidate. I studied eight subjects over six months and attempted all my exams together in one go at the age of 15, alhumdulilah. During this time, all other activity was on hold.

It was different for each of us though, as my siblings couldn't cope with so much pressure, they did theirs over two years with Oxford Home Schooling. (www.oxfordhomeschooling.co.uk)

I had initially applied to Umm UlQura University Makkah for medical sciences, but did not get a response from them. Therefore, I enrolled at Islamic Online University for a Bachelor of Arts in Islamic Studies. I also completed my Ijaza in Hifz E Quran from Global Quran Memorization Center.

Zawjah Ali: What is your mother's qualification?
Areeba Zubair: She has an MA in Home Economics.

Zawjah Ali: What has been her biggest strength and support in making homeschooling possible?
Areeba Zubair: Her iman and taqwa. MashaAllah. My mother is an inspirational lecturer, trainer and teacher who has lovingly changed and motivated people in preserving their

relationship with Allah. I think it is Allah's (swt) special blessing on her that she is always able to achieve her goals. My father has been very supportive of her ideas and plans. They shared a vision and struggled to make their children a means of coolness of their eyes. My mother's main concern has always been the Aakhira. She never gets upset over loss of dunya things.

Zawjah Ali: You are settled, a hafidah, successful mashaallah, what is the driving force behind this all?
Areeba Zubair: Haza min fazli rabbi. My parent's efforts, duas and constant motivation

Zawjah Ali: How has homeschooling helped you in becoming what you are today?
Areeba Zubair: Homeschooling saves you a lot of time to indulge in other activities and to pursue your passions.

Zawjah Ali: Would the same outcome have been possible by traditional schooling?
Areeba Zubair: No. I think it wouldn't be since you follow a very different, non-flexible routine.

Zawjah Ali: Do you think homeschooling would affect social skills of kids in higher studies especially if they are male kids?
Areeba Zubair: Might be to an extent. My brother did go to college for his A levels. He has now applied to study Islamic sciences at Madina University, Saudi Arabia.

Zawjah Ali: How did your mother cater to the need of friends and socialization during homeschooling years during graduation level?
Areeba Zubair: The Quran classes that were held at home were our little socialization platform. My mother is a very sociable person, and she often organized classes, lectures, and parties at home. We have a lot of family friends. A few years ago, she started Al Falaah Institute where my sister and I volunteered to teach kids at Sunday school, conduct workshops, made presentations, did counseling for students, etc. It was a project with over 150 students and their mothers. This gave us the opportunity to interact with kids of different ages and enhanced our speaking skills, teaching skills, and social skills. As it is said, 'When there is a will there is way'. With constant battle and aid of Allah, every situation can be turn to our own favor.

Three Teenagers, Three Approaches

By Brooke Benoit

I'm trying to recall why I had hoped that my children would attend an institutionalized high school after being homeschooled for their primary years. I preferred to avoid early academics, rather than placing them in school and then deschooling them to homeschool, but I suppose I had thought that going to high school would make it easier for them to transition to college. They would have the chance to learn how classroom settings work as well as all the administrative tasks, and they would experience a more rigid schedule than we have as homeschoolers. So far, none of my three older children have had any interest in going to a high school, even though they sometimes toyed with the idea when they were younger.

Sure we could nag, shove and force them to go, but that seems counter intuitive to why we homeschool in the first place. And especially to unschooling. Here is how each of my three teen sons is currently being homeschooled for high school and beyond.

Number One

We lived in a rural village in the High Atlas mountains when my first son became old enough to begin high school. Prior to that he had done various activities and used tutors for languages, but never a set curriculum. We enrolled in an offsite program I learned about in The Teenage Liberation Handbook, the accredited Clonlara high school in the US, where he could earn a US high school diploma. We were able to customize the program to his personal interests. He earned credit for raising animals, repairing bicycles, writing magazine articles, and hiking. I thought this was an incredible opportunity. He wasn't so convinced. It didn't feel like school/learning to him. Even when I designed more conventional courses with a textbook and supplemental material he felt like we were "cheating". After a year and half of this he agreed it would be best to study for his GED (General Education Diploma) rather than slowly earning his credits towards a diploma. So thereafter we moved to a city where he could take language courses locally, giving him a feel for how a school setting operates. He also went back to using a tutor for math.

Without taking any other formal classes and with little preparation he passed his GED tests, alhumdulillah. He is still undecided about his ultimate goal but is considering simultaneously attending a US community college online while studying for his SATs. He may also have to study for an entrance exam when he decides on his final major and college. If he transfers to or applies for a specific college that interests him here in Morocco he will have to improve his French for their entrance exam.

Number Two

My second son was eager to be enrolled in a program similar to the one the eldest tried, thank God. This school year he was old enough for ninth grade, and we had agreed to enroll him in Clonlara's distance program, where he would be assigned a teacher and curriculum rather than my doing all the customization and management. At the final hour, just before registering, he and I agreed that a full workload would be overwhelming for him, so again I set up a customized program. He is now taking English, math, an Arduino programming course, book illustration, Taekwondo, and art. Still a full workload, but with more flexible scheduling, and of course appealing to his current interests. We had agreed that next year he would register in the distance program, in which he would be assigned a teacher and full course load. He has a university in mind and is following closely their admittance guidelines.

After witnessing my first son pass the GED, my second son took closer notice of his school choice's insistence that the applicants do not need a high school diploma or GED. ACT and SAT scores, as well as a strong portfolio is what interests them. It was then that my son decided to ditch his diploma plans; instead he will focus on preparing for his ACT and SAT tests while building a portfolio, including by taking classes at online schools his preferred school suggests, such as EPGY, Stanford University's Education Program for Gifted Youth, and Open Course Ware. Again, I am excited for my child that he has chosen his own unique and exciting path, and I continue to facilitate his education as much as I possibly can.

Number Three

My third son is eager to catch up to and/or surpass his brothers. He has been pestering me about when I will enroll him in high school like I did them, except that he isn't old enough! He has used Khan Academy regularly for a few years and recently started working with a math and language tutor, but that still didn't appease him. Although I was reluctant as it seemed too game-ish to me, I have enrolled him in Time4Learning.com. He is enjoying working his way through the levels, though I suspect this will only briefly hold him at bay. Perhaps I will have an interesting update for Fitra Journal six months from now.

With four more children advancing towards their high school years, I don't doubt that each will have a unique experience. I look forward to watching them develop into young, capable adults, insha Allah, who can make their own decisions and change course when they recognize that they need to.

Unpacking This Unschooling Idea

By Zakiya Mahomed-Kalla

I call this article unpacking, because that's exactly what I've had to do to get my head around this huge, out-there idea called "unschooling". Ironically though, this methodology it is not 'out-there' to many unschooling parents. Of course some experienced unschooling as making a huge jump to a radically different educational method. But most see it as the most natural process in the world. So what is unschooling, exactly? Homeschooling expert Patrick Farenga describes unschooling as "interest driven, child-led, natural, organic, eclectic, or self-directed learning". Unschoolers are often seen as homeschoolers without a fixed curriculum.

But how do unschoolers learn anything?
Idzie Desmarais, grown unschooler and blogger at "I'm unschooled. Yes, I can write." sums it up beautifully: "I learn from: wandering, wondering, listening, reading, watching, discussing, running, writing, daydreaming, searching, researching, meditating, hibernating, playing, creating, growing, doing, helping, and everything else that comprises the day to day happenings of my life. For an unschooler, life is their classroom."

Where did unschooling come from?
The word 'unschool' appeared in the Oxford dictionary in 1994, though the concept unschooling as we know it was coined by John Holt, an ex-school teacher, in the late 90s who began advocating homeschooling in 1977. The idea that formal schooling is inadequate has been widespread for some time, as Mark Twain said, "I have never let my schooling interfere with my education." This just about sums up why unschoolers are opting out of the traditional schooling system all together. "Education" is derived from the Latin educatus – to rear, lead forth, and bring out something latent. *(Merriam-Webster.com)*

Education should be a way of learning that brings out the natural, God-given abilities, and interests of each individual. Instead, school classrooms the world over try to contain this natural learning, and re-package it in a uniform, prescribed product that is passed down the production line to colleges and universities, and then on to the world of employment. They function on a single curriculum for everybody, attempting to produce what education expert Sugata Mitra calls 'identical people'.

The problem with this is that the individuality and curiosity of natural learning is stifled and squashed. Children are told to be quiet, listen attentively, obey, and complete tasks (mostly written) in order to learn new concepts. Some teachers will allow discussion and respond to their students' questions, but only as much as time and the syllabus allow. The subjects that a school offers are the only choices that students have, and the content set by education departments are the limits within which they'll discover each subject. Further research, discovery, and real-life experience are dependent on the time available, the willingness of the teacher to allow these, and the general operating system of their school environment. Should students want to further explore a certain subject or theme within that subject, they'll have to do it outside of school time. Currently in South Africa (and many other parts of the world), homework and extra tuition mean that children barely have time for relaxation, let alone exploring their own interests!

All these restrictions kill students' intrinsic motivation to learn, and lead to the general attitude we know children to have about school – one of dislike and disinterest. The only way we get them to buy into school is through coercion, pressure to "achieve", and fear of failure. When these conflicts become too much for teachers and parents to cope with, we resort to blame, or "dumbing kids down" with medication. "When the child loses interest because their creativity has been canned, and they're being forced to learn what they don't want to learn, we say they have a learning problem," Jan Hunt, interviewed for Amy Childs' website "Supporting the Unschooling Life."

Why not alternate schooling?
Self-directed homeschooling, some Waldorf-style schools, and democratic schools such as the Philly Free School in the US, and Villa Monte in Switzerland, where children decide how or what they want to learn each day, and where standardised testing and report cards don't exist, are all alternatives to traditional schooling. And the options are on the rise, particularly in the online space. So why are there still unschoolers?

Unschooling parent of two boys, Ben Hewitt (interview: Outsideonline.com) says that the only reason they didn't opt for a Waldorf school was the cost: as much as $30,000 USD per year. The Hewitt's tried to incorporate Waldorf learning methods with one of their sons at home, which failed miserably. After tears and frustration, they abandoned all attempts at planting resources in his path, only to realise that "the moment we quit trying to teach our son anything was the moment he started really learning." Like Ben's story, just about every resource I've read, and every parent I've spoken to about unschooling, has come to this conclusion: children are natural learners. Give children the resources, leave them to explore and discover, and they will.

But is it adequate?
Discovering unschooling has been a strange and wonderful journey for me as an ex-school teacher. When I first heard about it, two things worried me (more actually, but these are the most significant) – how will these children be socialised, and how will they learn what they need to learn? The first one is a concern with homeschooling in general, and the second specific to unschooling.

So, I did some digging into the personal lives of unschoolers, asked what friends they have, and what diversity they can possibly experience being at home all day. And the answers have been refreshing. Sarah Parker* is part of an online network called Unschoolers in South Africa, where unschooling parents post resources, share concerns, support each other, and set up excursions and activities for unschoolers. They have monthly and bi-monthly meets to go ice-skating and ten-pin bowling, and their kids attend sewing, knitting, and cooking classes per their individual interests. Many unschoolers are active Scouts members, and others volunteer at their local churches and mosques, or soup kitchens, to name but a few "extra-curricular" activities. So arguably, unschoolers are more socially integrated than many schoolers I know!

As for learning what they need to learn, the question I've been asked in return is this – who decides what "needs" to be learned anyway? In the conventional system it is the state we live in, the education "authorities" who decide what the curriculum requirements are, and who dictate much of the content. The quality of learning is determined by standardised testing, and report cards reflect student progress and abilities.

Children must read by a certain age and be able to solve a certain level of math problems by another…the three R's are the order of the day – reading, writing, and arithmetic. As a teacher in this system, I see the flaws of one-size-fits-all education, but I have trouble imagining a world where if a child doesn't want to learn to read, no matter their age…they don't. On this point, Alan Smith*, father of three unschoolers, asks, "Why should a 7 year old be literate? So they can do their school work, there is no other domain in which this skill is necessary for a 7 year old." This is the gamble that unschooling parents take in the process of unschooling – all learning is needs based, and self-directed. I'm told that when a child finds him/herself in a situation where they need to read or write, and they want it badly enough, they will teach themselves how to do it, or seek out help to acquire the skill. This is what happened when Sarah Parker had to stop homeschooling her son Ismaeel* during her other son's debilitating illness.

Ismaeel spent whole days at home or at work with his dad, which involved several hours of Playstation games. While playing via a shared server, Ismaeel began receiving texts from a new-found friend, and wanted to be able to read and respond quickly, on his own. So he taught himself how to read by trial and error, asking his dad for help when he needed it. To his mother's amazement, when she turned to focus on his education again, she discovered that unschooling had found its way into her home, and let it stay.

Sadaf Farooqi, whose unschooling son has explored sewing and is now into electrical circuitry, is not concerned with his disinterest in reading. She believes that we all have different learning styles, and that the parent must observe each child's learning style and encourage it. Her son's is simply more hands-on than book-based. He'll learn to read when life pushes him to do so.

As for opportunities in higher education, locally and abroad, there are bridging courses, apprenticeships and internships, and various ways and means to meet the required standards for entrance as an unschooler. Unschoolers often excel in higher education and the working world, owing to their greater "real" life experience, which is welcomed. Professor of Educational Technology at Newcastle University, Sugata Mitra, believes that all children need to learn is broadband (internet), collaboration, and encouragement. Which forces me to ask - can't we all provide that at home?
  *Name changed at request of contributor

For more information on unschooling visit:
- http://sandradodd.com/unschool/definition.html
- http://www.johnholtgws.com/frequently-asked-questions-abo/
- http://yes-i-can-write.blogspot.co.za/

Charlotte Mason Method: Respecting Children's Unique Nature

By Dr Gemma Elizabeth

Going into home education, my primary focus was excellence: how can I make sure that my children get the best grades? How can they reach their full academic and spiritual potential? It wasn't enough that they were progressing, but they had to be progressing faster and better than their peers at school. They had to be the best!

I don't know what it was that dramatically changed my focus. Perhaps it was the realisation that the value of my children is more than just grades and exam results. Perhaps I realised that using my children as a means to compete with others is a dangerous and even wicked way to parent any child. Maybe it was just the answer to my duas, a prayer that I say often to my Lord, "Oh Allah, make me into the mother my children need me to be."

My outlook on motherhood and parenting has drastically altered over the years. My children are no longer empty vessels needing to be filled with my knowledge. Instead I understand that Allah ﷻ has created each of them as unique individuals. He ﷻ has crafted them as He sees fit, and no moulding or shaping from me will ever alter that. They will be who they are meant to be!

This newfound respect for my children, their personalities, their passions, and their very souls, has led me to embrace the homeschooling methodology of Miss Charlotte Mason, a revolutionary British educator from the twentieth century. Her method of home education comes naturally to our family and fits into our daily life with ease.

Although Charlotte Mason was a Christian, I have found the principles of her methodology align well with the Islamic understanding of the nature of children.

In the remainder of this article, I will share some of the key principles of the Charlotte Mason Method of Homeschooling, and explain why these ideologies resonate so strongly with me. The wording in Italics are direct quotes from Charlotte Mason herself.

1. "Children are born persons."
Charlotte Mason also believed that children were born as whole people, not empty vessels that needed to be shaped and moulded into what their parents deem suitable. Our children's souls have been entrusted to us by Allah ﷻ, and the nature of that soul is only known to Allah. Charlotte Mason said, "They are not born either good or bad, but with possibilities for good and for evil." This strongly correlates with the Islamic understanding of Fitra.

The Prophet ﷺ is reported to have said, "Each child is born in a state of Fitra, but his parents make him a Jew or a Christian." With regards to the foetus in the womb, the Prophet (pbuh) said, "The angel is commanded to write four words: his provision, his lifespan, his deeds, and whether he will end up wretched or joyful." The Charlotte Mason methodology understands that children have their own personalities, their own strengths and weaknesses, and ultimately, their own "destiny".

2. "Education is an atmosphere, discipline and life."
The Charlotte Mason method recognises that education is not just about informing the mind, but rather educating the whole child. In this famous quote, Charlotte Mason defines education in three parts: Atmosphere, Discipline and Life. The first part recognises the importance of the home, what she calls the "atmosphere." The environment we provide our children has a tremendous impact on them, as does our own example. Charlotte Mason explains further, "The ideas that rule your life make up the atmosphere around you." What ideas rule your life? Are your ideas and home conducive to the intellectual and spiritual growth of your children?

In the second part of this quote she mentions discipline. The Charlotte Mason method places great importance on instilling good character and manners in children. The Prophet (SAW) is reported to have said, "There is no gift that a parent can give his child that is better than good manners."

Finally, she mentions that education is a "life." By this she means that education should be applicable to the body, the intellect, and the soul. Teaching should be varied, with a wide variety of subjects to appeal to all aspects of the child's being. She said, "We allow no separation to grow up between the intellectual and 'spiritual' life of children," thereby encouraging educators not to teach religion as a separate subject, but rather incorporate it into every aspect of the school day.

3. Respect their Intelligence
It seems with every decade that passes, the quality of children's literature sharply declines, and with that children's vocabulary diminishes, their ability to articulate themselves decreases, as does their enjoyment for reading as a pastime. Charlotte Mason said, "They must grow up upon the best. There must never be a period in their lives when they are allowed to read or listen to twaddle or reading-made-easy." The term twaddle can refer to any material that "talks-down" to a child, dilutes the story, and under-values the intelligence of the child. Many examples of such books can be seen lining the shelves of supermarkets right at young children's eye level! She continues, "All who know children know that they do not talk twaddle and do not like it, and prefer that which appeals to their understanding." Instead, Mason encourages parents to fill their homes with books of value, where the storyline and characters have real depth, where the vocabulary is rich, where good moral values are

taught, and the story excites your children's imagination. Examples of these would be classic children's literature such as Pinocchio, The Secret Garden, and The Tales of Winnie-The-Pooh to name a few.

4. "Never be within doors when you can rightly be without."

There has been increasing evidence that aspects of today's lifestyle can be greatly detrimental to the health and mental well-being of our children. Richard Louv, best-selling author of Last Child in the Woods says, "Now, more than ever, we need nature as a balancing agent." Sue Palmer, author of "Toxic Childhood" says, "Free outdoor play is where we acquire the emotional skills to see us through the rest of our lives. The self-confidence that grows from solving our own problems. The self-esteem that swells when, having feared you're lost, you still find the way home….. Seems to me that denying children the opportunity to learn all these lessons and acquire all these skills is a risk not worth taking." Charlotte Mason, despite being born almost 100 years before the television was invented, recognised the benefit of outdoor play. Her method of home education encourages mothers to take their children outdoors for several hours everyday. She says, "It is infinitely well worth the mother's while to take some pains every day to secure, in the first place, that her children spend hours daily amongst rural and natural objects; and, in the second place, to infuse into them, or rather, to cherish in them, the love of investigation..."

5. No Formal Teaching Before Seven Years-old

Charlotte Mason strongly believed that formal education should not begin until the child is six or seven years of age. She says, "…the chief function of the child--his business in the world during the first six or seven years of his life--is to find out all he can, about whatever comes under his notice, by means of his five senses; that he has an insatiable appetite for knowledge got in this way; and that, therefore, the endeavour of his parents should be to put him in the way of making acquaintance freely with Nature and natural objects…" The concept of delaying formal education is not as strange as it may seem. In Sweden and Finland, where formal schooling does not begin until seven years-old, measures have indicated that children have greater academic achievement and general well-being compared to children the U.K., where schooling begins at 4 years-old. Likewise, many Muslim scholars, when speaking on the topic of educating children, often quote Ali ibn Abu Talib ؓ who famously said, "Play with them for the first seven years (of their life); then teach them for the next seven years; then advise them for the next seven years (and after that)."

I am by no means suggesting that the Charlotte Mason method was or is an Islamic approach to home-education. However, as a Muslim mother, it resonates with me and correlates with many principles that Islam has already set out. The Charlotte Mason approach shows respect to the body, intellect, and essence of the child. It teaches that the role of a mother is to encourage and nurture the good in their children, and help them to become the best version of who God created them to be.

As I have come to understand the nature of my children, and my role as their mother, I have experienced a growing respect for them. I cannot help but admire their ability to learn and grasp new ideas so readily. Their passion for learning is contagious and their innocent desire to "do the right thing" constantly inspires me to be a better mother, and a better person. What could be more worthy of my respect than that?

Avoiding The Pitfalls of Part-Time Homeschooling

By Asma Ali

When I tell people I part-time homeschool my boys, I'm usually met with intrigue and surprise. In all honesty, I was unaware that such a schooling arrangement existed until I moved to Saudi Arabia and began homeschooling. So what exactly is it?

Also known as flexi-schooling or part-time enrollment, part-time homeschooling usually involves your child attending regular school for part of the day or week and studying at home for the rest. Although legal, regulations for this set up depend on the school board and vary from area to area. This type of schooling is reported to be on the rise in the UK, but is also very common amongst expat families living in Saudi Arabia. Children are typically sent to a tahfeedh (a school with a focus on hifdh) with the rationale they will be memorizing the Qur'an whilst being immersed in the Arabic language and culture. As schools here finish at a relatively early time of 1:15 pm, kids can complete a full day in class without having to be pulled out during the week. A normal weekday can appear very straightforward: children are home by lunch and still have the afternoon to spare. Although this may sound like a dream scenario, part-time homeschooling has a unique set of challenges that can very quickly turn it into a nightmare! More so when living abroad as there is the added concern to ensure your children are receiving an adequate education in English.

The term "part-time" itself is terribly deceptive as it still requires all the commitment and effort you would expect with traditional homeschooling; do not be fooled into thinking this is an "easy" option, it is anything but. However, that does not mean it is unmanageable. Over the years, I have come to recognize common obstacles that would initially leave me feeling stressed and drowning in failed expectations. The following are a few ideas on how to overcome these problems and some top tips from friends in the same boat. With a little preparation for such pitfalls, there is no reason why part-time homeschooling should not be an incredibly rewarding and advantageous situation.

Time

The most obvious and challenging aspect about part-time homeschooling is the amount of time you actually have to get anything done. When you factor in time to unwind and play, homework (yes, such is life with school) and hifdh, there really is not that much of it. I am a big believer in the old adage that if you fail to plan, you plan to fail. This can be applied to all areas of life, but with homeschooling, it is crucial to have a plan or schedule of some sort so you have an idea of exactly what it is you are hoping to achieve that day/week/month.

• Set aside some time to think about academic goals for the year (be realistic!) and work out what you need to be doing to attain them. Break this down to monthly planning. To avoid outlining a schedule every night, I spend an evening every other week drafting a plan – I find it helpful to jot down what I intend to do with each child on each day and what resources I will be using. You can make it as detailed as you like or just a rough sketch, whatever works for you. You might prefer to do a weekly plan, but it's probably best not to go over two weeks as even the best-laid plans go awry! Life happens, which means you can get a little behind schedule. And that's ok. I have finally gotten past the pressure I would feel for not completing intended tasks. The whole point of creating a plan is to provide some direction, not extra burden. Pencil plans in and if it doesn't happen, just try again the following day.

• Keep a cut-off time to your schooling. I personally find the kids less receptive after a certain hour and so any form of learning becomes an uphill battle. It also helps to determine how long I will spend on a given topic and how long for breaks.

• Parents who are also focused on doing hifdh with their children often struggle to fit it all in. Despite memorizing at school in Saudi, time always needs to be made to revise and consolidate at home. Umm Abdullah, a homeschooling mum of two, says, "This is the first thing we concentrate on once the kids have eaten and changed. The incentive is that we get the most important task of the day done early so there is more barakah in our time."

Creativity

The lack of creativity in my teaching style was something that always bothered me and it is something I am still working on; it was hard enough ensuring I was providing the right materials without worrying if things were entertaining! However, it is useful to remember that creativity in education is not only fun and engaging, but nurtures a love of learning.

My eldest son is what I tend to call a "solid learner." He was always quite happy to simply work his way through a bunch of textbooks and be done with it. His brother, however, is the complete opposite, and I was forced to leave my comfort zone of working from books and apply a little imagination. To my delight, I discovered that making things a little more interesting does not have to take much time at all and fewer textbooks actually simplifies things.

Let me just clarify this does not mean if you are solely using textbooks you are doing something wrong. Creative methods of learning provides an alternative that plays to a child's strength; not only is creativity natural to them, it can provide a breath of fresh air to daily schooling.

• Try heading into the kitchen to bake together! This is a great way to introduce and reinforce addition, multiplication, measurement and fractions.

- Scholastic has a wonderful resource that uses Lego to help build math concepts - http://www.scholastic.com/teachers/top-teaching/2013/12/using-lego-build-math-concepts

- Look into unit studies for older children: teaching a wide range of subjects through one point of interest. When part-time homeschooling, it is difficult to manage more than two or three subjects so these are usually limited to English, math and science. Depending on what you choose, a unit study gives the opportunity to incorporate subjects like history, geography, art, etc.

- Spend more time on creative writing. It is a surefire way to improve spelling, punctuation, and grammar than a regular English lesson.

- Transformation! Bazigha, mum of four, came up with a particularly ingenious way to teach her younger brood: "I lacked patience when teaching my daughter how to read so I decided to transform myself into 'Abla Nada!' She was a character I created who dressed like a teacher, did not get upset and was very pleasant. My idea worked! My daughter fell in love with her and enjoyed learning with 'her' so I continued on the act when teaching the rest of my children."

Energy and mood

The reality for part-time schooled children in Saudi is that they are still spending a full day at school so they arrive home tired, hungry, and often in no mood to study any further. With this in mind, I try to keep lessons short – sometimes I spend no more than 15 minutes - and have time for a break in between subjects. Acknowledge that homeschooling can be tough at the best of times and go easy on yourself and your children. Find something that motivates them and lightens their mood when they come home.

- Encourage downtime. After school, kids want nothing more than to play and with a busy schedule they really need to unwind. It can be helpful to let them spend just a little time on something of their choosing before doing any work. Flitting from one activity to another can also be draining. Umm Abdullah battles tiredness by encouraging her boys to relax on the way home from school. "Once they get in the car, I tell them to put their seats back, close their eyes, and do not talk! If they fall asleep for a short while, alhamdulillah, and if not, then at least they have rested before getting home."

- Try a reward system. This is my favorite way to avoid a complete meltdown on the days where a little more math is less than appealing; my children love knowing there is a daily reward awaiting them once they have completed their activities. This ranges from time on the Xbox to watching their favorite cartoon or even a little extra time to read before bed. Reward charts are also helpful where they gain an agreed amount of stars during the week before earning a prize.

- Make use of online learning. Remember the importance of getting creative? There are some great educational websites around that make learning fun! Kids are more enthusiastic when doing something a little different and will happily sit with the laptop to play games that constitute a lesson! Najma, mum of three, brings out the console for a spot of physical education – "My boys absolutely love playing Wii sports. I much prefer them being active rather than sitting in front of the computer as the exercise they get from playing is proven to enhance thinking skills. Win-win all round."

There is no doubt that homeschooling can be a real challenge and the circumstances in Saudi can make it all the more overwhelming. But with enough dedication and forethought, the journey can become a lot smoother and more enjoyable. There are still times I panic and wonder if I am doing enough (or even too much!) but overall, striking a balance means we can get the best of both worlds.

Memory Tips and Tricks for Effective Learning

By Zawjah Ali

A few days back I met my old school friend and delighted to learn about an upcoming reunion of school friends. I asked for her cell number and kept repeating it out loud until I could pen it down. In my attempt to find a paper and pen, I was surprised that I nearly forget the number! Just like everyone else, my working memory needs to be trained and tamed.

Memory is our ability to encode, store, and retrieve information. It has three types:
• Sensory memory is the shortest-term element of memory. It is the ability to retain impressions of sensory information after the original stimuli have ended.

• Short-term memory (also called "primary" or "active memory") is the capacity for holding, but not manipulating, a small amount of information in the mind in an active, readily available state for a short period of time.

• Long-term memory (LTM) is the final stage of the dual memory model proposed in the Atkinson-Shiffrin memory model, in which information can be stored for long periods of time. While short-term and working memory persist for only about 18 to 30 seconds, information can remain in long-term memory indefinitely.

Our day-to-day activities that we do systematically is part of our LTM. Driving a car is a procedural memory which comes under the umbrella term of LTM.

Knowing all these details can help homeschooling parents decide the best suited strategy to engage their children's (and their own) minds more efficiently. In some cases one style is best to be used, and at other times a combo of two different styles. Homeschooling is the best place to cater to the individual needs. It is not like school decorum which is set for all students, neglecting their varied study styles.

These three levels and the involved processing can be effective by using memory aids and strategies. Before that one must know which type of learner one is.

Visual learners prefer to watch demonstrations. Their ability to visualize images is strong and their concentration is intense. They tend to remember faces well as compared to names. For young children, colorful visual cues such as vibrant board books and pictorial books which have appealing imagery can aid in strengthening memory. For high schoolers, the things which aid in this learning include: writing down notes, use of highlighters and sticky notes, repetition, and self-study.

Auditory Learners tend to remember well when information is given in a memorable tone and is repeated out aloud. Younger children grasp more when info is given in chants and rhymes. For older kids, class discussions, reading out aloud, storytelling, verbal analogies, jingles, and mnemonic devices are helpful.

Physical learners or tactile kinesthetic learners learn best by doing. They need direct involvement. The opportunities to touch and feel are their greatest aids in learning. As babies, they rely on their ability to touch to grasp new ideas. This is why stress is made on the use of sensory bins and toys for tots. For older children, use of posters in their work space, learning or repeating when on exercise bike, taking adventure trips, graphic note-taking such as mapping and concept trees, using different positions for studying such as standing desks, and hands-on experiments are helpful.

So how can a combo of two or all learning types be achieved? Technology use can help in using all senses to comprehend and learn as it offers multi-sensory details. Tablets with e-textbooks are a combined use of both multisensory and multimedia. But e-textbooks do not diminish the importance of auditory learning insists John Black, Cleveland E. Dodge Professor in the Department of Human Development at Teachers College, Columbia University.

Learning requires all senses to work. A study revealed that auditory memory is trumped by visual memory. The Chinese adage which says "I hear I forget, I see I remember" is favored by a study done by Associate professor of psychology and neuroscience Amy Poremba and graduate student James Bigelow. The aid of digital devices is a menace for some. It all depends on the users. Excessive use of anything is hazardous, even the excessive sweetness is venom. Our kids get addicted to these gadgets and it badly affects their attention span and memory. Use of the memory devices along with these technologies is a better option.

There are many memorization aids available which can be used easily according to which best suits our learning styles. These include:

Mnemonics
When a person is given any large string of words, he will only be able to retain the first few and last few which is known as "the recency and latency effect." To increase the capacity to learn the whole string, a technique is to be used. Mnemonics is when you take the first letter of each word to remember what the whole chain stands for. For instance to remember the colors of the rainbow there is the mnemonic device, such as "VIBGYOR" (violet, indigo, blue, green, yellow, orange, red) in Pakistan, opposite of "ROY G BIV" in the US. This works best for chemistry too.

Chunking
When a large amount of data is grouped to enhance learning more effectively this is called "chunking." How telephone numbers are written and repeated is an example of this

technique.

Rehearsing
My psychology teacher told us to make posters and stick them to the walls of our bathroom! Learning medical terminologies is difficult and the bathroom is a place we all visit often. According to her this will provide continuous revision and stimuli to learn. Bright, vivid posters with flow charts make it easy to remember and form chains.

Teach
I remember, during my days of schooling, I would write and teach to my imaginary students as exercises in role playing. Teaching is the best means of retaining and transferring your learned material to your long term memory. It also helps you to tap the areas where there is still some confusion for you to seek clarity on a subject. Peer tutoring is a great way for children to learn.

Funny associations
I also used to learn the characteristics of disorders by linking them to people around me. This humorous device helped me immensely to memorize. Later, at time of recall, thinking of the person would automatically give me the list of characteristics.

Learning should never be boring. It becomes a hassle when we impose it on ourselves and our kids in uncreative, ill-fitting ways. Homeschooling is a great opportunity to study and learn based on the hours of a child's receptiveness and eagerness to learn.

http://news.nationalgeographic.com/news/2014/03/140312-auditory-memory-visual-learning-brain-research-science/

How to Train Your Dragonfruit: 10 Reasons to Cook with Your Kids

By Klaudia Khan

Someone has recently told me that if you are a homeschooler and your teenage kids can't cook then you are pretty much a failure. My children may have a good few years to go before they enter their teenagerhood, but I'm eager to get them cooking as soon as possible, if not for the above reason, then certainly for the reasons below:

1. Cooking is a useful skill – a life skill if you prefer, and if your child learns to cook it certainly gives them a sense of achievement and independence, it's a boost to their confidence. The beginnings may be hard, (for you rather than for them) as they might be eager to cook, yet less so to clean, but if you persist and encourage them they will get there one day. And the day they accomplish their first cooking mission, in sha Allah, the proud smile on their face will be your reward. Learning to cook is much like learning to eat – it's awfully messy to begin with, but you have to let them do it and learn through practice, for their and your own good.

2. You are what you eat, and you eat what you cook – children who know how to cook, or at least fix themselves a sandwich, are less likely to stuff themselves with unhealthy processed packaged snacks. Also, if you let your children prepare the healthy stuff by themselves they are more likely to eat it. Sometimes it's just the case of finding the right recipe collection that would encourage them to try new things. So yeah, let them train their dragonfruit. Or broccoli. Or asparagus.

3. The kitchen is a brain-gym – cooking involves lots of activities that will help your children develop their hand-eye coordination and fine motor skills: stirring, mixing, kneading, pouring... and that's just the warm ups!

4. Recipes are to be read – all my children love cookbooks, even my 18-month-old daughter loves leafing through them occasionally pointing to things that she knows well, like some fruit. When kids see you reading while cooking they want to copy that and for them reading and understanding recipes is great literacy training. For the younger ones you can start with pictorial cookbooks, like Pretend Soup or Silver Spoon for Children. Let older kids read the whole recipe before they start and prepare all they need. You can also ask them to briefly tell you what needs to be done.

5. Counting your five-a-day – cooking requires lots of mathematics: counting, dividing, adding and sharing, measuring and even geometry – have you tried halving your square toast in more than one way? You don't have to put special effort to get your children to practice their math in the kitchen – just let it be a natural part of food preparation; practical math put to the right use.

6. Science is a cupcake – from exploring the changing state of water, to the mystery of the raising dough, there is plenty of science to explore in the kitchen. Your kids can discover lots by themselves and you might just need to help them find the right words to describe what they see. If you need some ideas try http://www.science-sparks.com/2013/04/27/kitchen-science-round-up/ or Kitchen Science Lab for Kids: 52 Family Friendly Experiments from Around the House by Liz Lee Heinecke.

7. Management, cooperation and troubleshooting – of course cooking requires lots of management: you have to take make sure first that you have all you need, then manage the time, and often do many things at once! And if there is someone cooking with you, even better – you get a chance to learn cooperation. Baking powder is all gone? What can we do now? Is there a substitute or shall we run to the corner shop? That's called troubleshooting.

8. Exotic flavours – everybody knows pizza, but do your children know where it originates from? Once you go through your Italian recipes (always the favorites in children's books) maybe it's time to try something more exotic? Food can be a great pretext to learning geography. Wherever you live you are most likely using ingredients from different countries, if only spices. Try tracking the origin of all the ingredients on your plate, or try cooking a single origin dish. The possibilities are plenty! And a map of the world on the kitchen wall would also come in handy...

9. Imaginary flavours and art on the plate – cooking sparks imagination! Decorating cupcakes is an obvious form of creativity in the kitchen, but there is so much more you can do. Decorating any biscuits (cookies) or cakes requires some artistry, but you can do the same with sandwiches. Older children can get creative with salads or try their hand at composing themed menus for family get-togethers. You can borrow an idea from a cooking competition and ask your teenagers to prepare a dish from seemingly odd ingredients.

10. Family time in the kitchen – when cooking with children you have to give them a lot of attention and they are going to love it! Don't teach them cooking, but engage and have fun together. Be prepared for the mess – cover carpeted areas with plastic sheets! – and give yourself plenty of time. Cooking together makes wonderful memories, and if you'd like some permanent record of the moments, create your own family cookbook, with recipes passed from great aunties and those you make up together, or your own versions of favorite dishes. Remember that how you spend time together is more important than the end result of your cooking.

Chapter 3
ORGANIZING AND RETHINKING THINGS

Whose Identity is it Anyway?

By Khalida Haque

"I think therefore I am."
-*Descartes*

Who we are is very important. Think back to a time, and this will be easy for anyone who is a mother or a woman, when a sense of self was lost. When you couldn't describe yourself, the things you liked or disliked or anything about yourself. How did you feel during that time? As human beings having a sense of ourselves, knowing who we are plays a fundamental role in what we contribute to this world and life.

What is Identity?
"I have been sent to perfect good character."
-The Prophet Muhammad (SAW)

Identity is the very essence of a person and it is intrinsically linked to character, which cannot be built or improved upon if we don't know who we are. Character, or rather perfecting it, is what our journey in life is all about and how we ought to be moving forward. Good character means we will aspire to do good which will ultimately draw us closer to Allah (SWT).

The concept of identity is a social construct in that we learn who we are through others. We piece together our identities or rather our senses of self through what is reflected to us as we grow. The question of who we are is answered by who we identify with, and who we identify with is dependent upon our parenting, background, and history. Basically our identity develops through what we are exposed to. There are a number of facets in relation to identity which play a huge part in determining how we understand the world as well as how we experience it. The main ones are: gender, social class, age, race, ethnicity, and in the case of Muslims the most important one is religion which ought to override the others. However, there is also a personal aspect to identity and that is the individual natural disposition which is most often referred to as "personality".

Why is identity important?
Having a sense of identity is crucial. It allows people to be distinct as individuals, to cultivate

a sense of well-being, significance and confidence, and to fit in with certain groups and cultures. If we don't know who we are we don't have a sense of belonging, which is of fundamental importance as we can see from Maslow's Hierarchy of Human needs below:

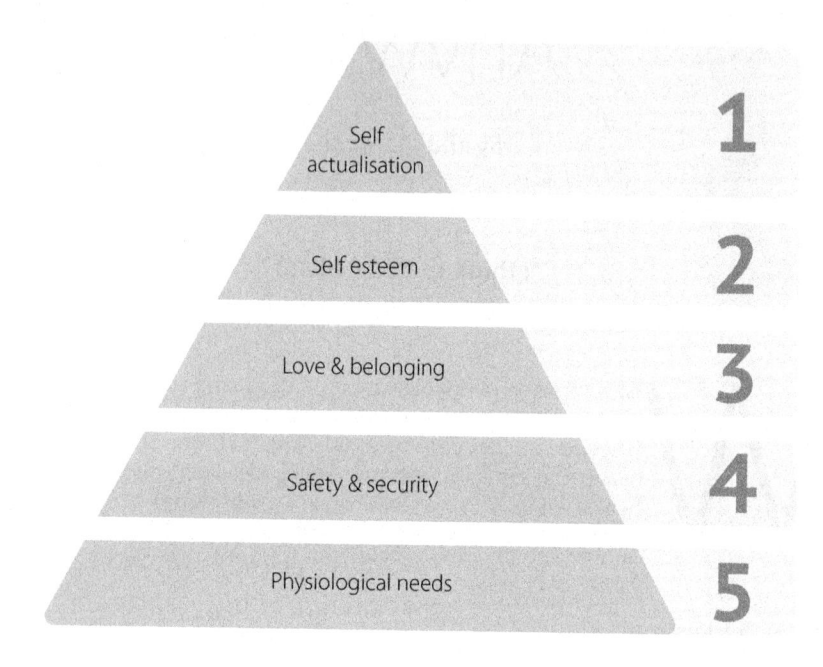

```
            /\
           /  \
          / Self \              1
         /actualisation\
        /--------------\
       /                \
      /   Self esteem    \     2
     /--------------------\
    /                      \
   /    Love & belonging    \  3
  /--------------------------\
 /                            \
/      Safety & security       \ 4
--------------------------------
/                                \
/      Physiological needs        \ 5
------------------------------------
```

The sense of belonging is borne out of the love we feel in relation to others. If this level of need is unfulfilled we cannot develop in terms of esteem and confidence and so we are unlikely to achieve in life and cultivate respect – both of others and received by others. And obviously if all of that is missing it is plausible that we will not self actualise to become who we have the potential to be. When we don't reach that potential how do we contribute to the world and its inhabitants? If identity is missing, or a very negative identity develops, we are likely to resort to abusive practices which we know will in turn create a toxic cycle. If we grow up in an environment with a lack of one or more of the human needs in Maslow's Hierarchy or they are in some way negatively provided we stand to produce an unhealthy internal working model.

Bowlby, who derived the concept of an internal working model, suggests that the primary caregiver (most often the parents) generate a template for future relationships through this model. The model has three main features: (1) a model of others as being trustworthy, (2) a model of the self as valuable, and (3) a model of the self as effective when interacting with others.

Having our human needs be satisfied as we grow and live our lives will influence how we see ourselves and others. Basically the gratification of these needs interplay with our sense of who we are and who we will identify ourselves with.

How do we nurture identity?
Now that the significance of identity has been understood, how do we ensure that a positive sense of self is nurtured? The characteristic that needs to be cultivated is resilience. Resilience is the ability to recover from difficult and adverse situations and experiences. What is it that develops this ability? Research has shown that, despite adversity, children who are valued and loved grow up resilient. If a child feels heard and valued, and is given decision-making power in relation to their lives, it will enhance other protective factors such as a strong belief system, supportive friendships, connection to our environment and community, and coping and social skills. All the aforementioned protective factors are there within our deen of Islam but it is how the deen is conveyed to our children as they grow which determines if those aspects develop.

In the world, certainly in the UK, there is currently too much emphasis on academic achievement and attaining top grades. This does not make for intelligence of any kind because the learning that is consequently done is to achieve certain results and not to understand a subject. The levels of anxiety and mental health issues in children are on the rise due to this focus as well as are increasing dysfunctional family relationships of various kinds.

Homeschoolers do not generally buy into the viewpoint that education and qualifications are a sign of intelligence. Homeschoolers tend to achieve better results than their school taught counterparts and at an earlier age. Moreover, they seem to also develop the resilience that we are exploring as well as other important life skills. This is not to say that all home schoolers develop this way and that all school taught children the other way. The main contributing factor to all these developments is parenting rather than where or how they are schooled. A child who is brought up in an environment of love and encouragement becomes a giving and can-do individual.

To nurture a good internal working model in a child is to be there, loving, present and consistent. This will then insha'Allah satisfy the hierarchy of needs leading them to self actualising and becoming who they are placed on Earth to be. Children are not our possessions or extensions of ourselves. Rather they are an amanah (trust) destined to do the things that Allah (SWT) has ordained. Even if you yourself have had a difficult and dysfunctional upbringing you can, through conscious choice, not pass that onto your children. If we can change ourselves and our patterns we can be sure that our children will pick up those good new patterns rather than our old ones.

"...Surely Allah changes not the condition of a people, until they change their own condition..."
(Qur'an 13:11)

Overcoming Self-Doubt and Second-Guessing

By Umm Yusuf Aisha Lbhalla

"**Why**" do you homeschool your kids?" is often asked of homeschooling parents. The answer to this question varies greatly from parent to parent. Deciding to homeschool is a decision based on a variety of reasons:

"We want a faith-driven environment."
"Low quality education, violence and bullying are rampant in the public school system."
"My child is gifted and needs an accelerated curriculum."
"I need to nurture my child's strengths and focus on the weaknesses."
"My child has difficulty learning or a different learning style."

Whatever the reasons are, deciding to homeschool is a courageous and challenging choice. A choice and commitment made for the child's benefit.

In my case, I was excited, determined, and sure that I would and could homeschool my sons. Then self-doubt and second-guessing crept in. *Am I qualified to teach my children, what if they miss out? Am I patient enough? Will my educational weaknesses be my children's weaknesses? What if my children hate homeschool, will they hate me for it?* As a parent, being solely responsible for your children's entire education is a stressful, intimidating notion that can stir up many doubts and emotions.

If you are having self-doubt and second guessing about homeschooling, know it is the norm and that you are not alone. While self-doubt is normal, allowing it to overly occupy your thoughts can and will chip away at your intentions, nip at your confidence, affect your decisions, and maybe ruin your homeschool experience.

To overcome my self-doubt I did a few things. I petitioned Allah ﷻ, I affirmed my intentions, I confirmed my reasons for homeschooling my sons, I adjusted my thinking, and I modified my overall approach towards homeschooling. Since doubts are rooted in fear, I had to remember what Allah ﷻ says about doubt, fear, and trust. He calls us to not worry, to put our trust in Him, to depend upon Him, and to seek support and help from Him:

"Then when you have decided on a course of action, put your trust in Allah: Allah loves those who put their trust in Him. If Allah helps you believers, no one can overcome you. If he forsakes

you, who else can help you? And in Allah alone let believers put their trust." - Qur'an 3: 159-160

The lessons of Prophet Musa ﷺ also encapsulates our need to constantly turn to Allah ﷻ for help and assurance. When tasked with delivering the message to the tyrant Pharaoh, Musa ﷺ said "My Lord! Expand for me by breast (with assurance). And ease for me my task. And untie the knot from my tongue. That they may understand my speech." *-Qur'an: 20: 25-28*

When Musa ﷺ and his people fled from Pharaoh and his troops, "And when the two hosts saw each other, the companions of Musa ﷺ said: 'We are sure to be overtaken. Musa ﷺ said: 'Nay, verily, with me is my Lord. He will guide me.'" *-Qur'an 26: 61-62*

Hands down, there is no one – absolutely no one in this world - that loves your child more than you. No one knows and understands your child more than you. And no one knows what is best for you child more than you. This, coupled with my desire to instill Islamic values in my sons and the hadith below, enabled me to affirm my intentions and reasons for homeschooling my sons. This even included formulating a mission statement designed to keep me focused on the main reasons for our homeschool journey, and to keep me encouraged during discouraging times.

Rasulullah ﷺ: "Every one of you is a shepherd and is responsible for his flock. The leader of people is a guardian and is responsible for his subjects. A man is the guardian of his family and he is responsible for them. A woman is the guardian of her husband's home and his children and she is responsible for them. The servant of a man is a guardian of the property of his master and he is responsible for it. No doubt, every one of you is a shepherd and is responsible for his flock." *- Bukhāri, Muslim*

Next, I adjusted my thinking and I modified my overall approach towards homeschooling. This included many elements with the most important being deciding that our homeschool is not and will not be a duplicate of public school in the home, nor should it be. Homeschool is supposed to be flexible, individualized, and free to cater to my children's specific needs, which makes it something that cannot be found in public schools. Additionally, our homeschool will not be like another sister's school, or a popular blogger's school. Our homeschool will be tailored to fit my children's needs, our family's pace, and my teaching style.

I then approached homeschooling with a view that it should be enjoyable, tear-free, and stress-free for the boys and me. This meant learning how to be flexible because unexpected things happen. My daily plan can be turned upside down in a second. An important phone call can delay class, a scheduled lesson was not completed, an emergency errand was made, etc. Life happens, accept that it is okay and that you and the kids will survive an "off" day. Also it is more important for my children to understand a subject then to finish just for finishing's sake. Retaining and understanding what they learn, and cultivating a curiosity and lifelong love for learning is more important to me than quantity alone.

There are no cookie cutter homeschooling families or children. Children have different needs and different learning styles, which may even include not having mommy's learning style and absorbing information like she does! Accepting this allowed me to be more patient and to free my mind from thinking *'they must complete these subjects and units based on their grade level'* even if they are struggling and clearly not ready.

I was a stickler about plans. And when I could not complete the day's lesson plan, I felt like a failure. While my curriculum is a useful planning tool, I no longer allow my curriculum to steer my every move, especially if a concept is not being grasped by my sons. Now, I give the boys a quick break during a difficult subject or use a different format to deliver the lesson. This has proven to be effective. And while I did not want my children to drift behind, I do not want to pressure them thereby making learning unenjoyable. This only results in tears and frustration for us both. hen a curriculum was not working out, I changed it for one that worked, and now we all enjoy the new curriculum.

These are just some of the changes I adopted in order to remove self-doubt and second-guessing from our homeschool. Remembering that homeschooling is a lifestyle, I don't seek perfection as I will never find it. Instead I seek progress, then celebrate and encourage that progress my children and I made. I no longer let self-doubt compound unrealistic expectations and unnecessary burdens thereby sabotaging our homeschool.

While it is important for me to have homeschooling goals for my children, it is even more important to remember that first and foremost these are little people, impressionable little people with a parent-child relationship at stake. I don't want to focus just on the end product while missing the beauty and joy of the homeschooling journey with my Beloveds. Homeschooling can be a rich and rewarding experience for both children and parents. Enjoy the journey together and make beautiful memories along the way.

Can You Be A Minimalist And Homeschool?

By Brooke Benoit

I can't. Many women admit that they don't want to homeschool because they enjoy keeping a tidy home. There are, of course, other factors which allow them to be able to make this seemingly callous statement, such as that they have access to schools that are somewhere between decent to excellent, or they have an issue with mess or clutter such as OCD. There are studies that link women's increased physiological stress levels to the "clutter" levels of their homes.* I'm going to assume this is because all of the family business of organization and cleaning usually lies squarely on a woman's shoulders. It is a huge and stressful undertaking. While some women can be frank about not being able to add on the workload and multiple jobs of running a school in your home, others, such as myself, may undervalue this aspect of homeschooling - *stuff* builds up, it accumulates everywhere for every subject, project and interest. And it stresses us out.

At the beginning of our homeschooling journey I did okay with managing stuff. Of course, I only had two little kids then so our stuff was mostly their budding collection of toys for multiple purposes (indoor, outdoor, etc), craft supplies, and my homeschooling texts: how-to-books and a little curriculum. As we had more children and acquired more things it became harder. We moved out of the country and then back again, so we didn't have all of the furniture that had taken years to accumulate. While the basics were first to be replaced - beds, tables, appliances- I remember longing for proper shelving and the joy I had when we were finally able to purchase a cabinet in which I could lock away our craft supplies from little hands.

I feel the tipping point of my own, and even my husband's, stress levels happened when I returned to school to finish my degree. While my husband had always cooked and hands-on cared for the children, he didn't deal with any of the organization tasks, such as buying near constantly needed new clothes, making and attending various appointments, thoroughly cleaning up all the toys and other kids' items by separating them, fixing them, and rotating them out. There were numerous tasks we both underestimated the time and skill it took to manage. When other homeschooling moms ask me about starting a home-based business I think back to this stressful time. What could I have done differently? Not much. This is another underestimated thing about homeschooling - we must remain flexible. Circumstances are constantly changing. Just when the ink dries on your perfected schedule, a tutor moves away, your transmission dies, you break a toe - life throws us hurdles at a constant pace.

Not having a showroom-ready house was another issue tied to all this stuff that came up later for us. This problem existed a little bit while we were living in the States, mostly when people would want to drop by and I felt that my home was in shambles compared to my guests who were not running a very active, hands-on, often messy school in their homes. For someone who has never experienced homeschooling in any way it can be shocking to walk into a kitchen which not only has the typical dish and cooking messes many of us would be tempted to hide under the sink, but there are also art and science projects in various stages of progress, maybe a computer desk where you would expect a dining area or a sand table - maybe an indoor gym! I've had guests who were unable to hide the shock on their face the first time they saw my home. Others made uninformed, hurtful statements about the state of my home.

When we moved to Morocco, where the term 'homeschool' isn't known at all, this issue became much more stressful. It's just unheard of to have so much stuff. Part of the well-known Moroccan hospitality is in having your home guest-ready at all times. As long as we have been homeschooling, I've never had the luxury of a guest bathroom where there isn't an occasional tell-tale sign of paint brushes having been rinsed in the sink or a pristine sitting room; our living room has long been needed as a play/work space for our children. Our clutter causes new kinds of stresses here in Morocco, including some guilt about having so much among people who have very little. Only the most expensive private schools I couldn't possible afford have a comparable amount and quality of educational tools we have, alhumdulillah.

Ultimately, we need stuff to homeschool. We need to try various styles and activities to educate and engage our children, and sometimes we will find some things that worked great taper off or suddenly stop working, and all of this is in various ways is tied to stuff, getting new stuff, repairing or replacing well-used stuff, getting rid of old stuff... These are my four best tips for minimizing the stuff stress.

1. Practice your self-talk
People are going to judge this appearance aspect of your lifestyle just as they do every other aspect. Remind yourself that your lifestyle and home *are different* and therefore *look different*. Remind yourself that you are doing the best you can in this unusual situation and that it is really okay to be different, it's best for you and your family. Then, of course, be sure you are doing your best with all your stuff.

2. Invest in organizing
You are essentially running a business. You need supplies, including some things to put all those supplies in and on. Be strategic about these purchases as they need to withstand the long haul. Think *institutional quality*. Among my must haves for homeschooling are work tables for the kids, strong shelving units and a lot of cabinetry to store (hide!) some of the clutter. I absolutely loathe poor quality plastic storage containers that crack and break within a few months, if not days, of buying them. I pick up rubber storage solutions whenever I find them here and also use a lot of different sized baskets. An important thing to keep in mind is that things that are not stored well will often get damaged or misplaced, purchasing organizing solutions is not a frivolous home makeover kind of thing at all, it prevents waste in the long run.

3. Delay purchases
Creating a homeschooling budget has been especially challenging for me as our income is low and fluctuates, alhumdulillah. It's ideal to have a budget though. One budget trick I often use is to avoid spontaneous purchases, which are super easy to make when you are homeschooling. Just about everything can be used for educational purposes! And your kids will introduce you to so many interests you have never explored before, you are going to be tempted a lot. Make a rule not to buy things on the spot, rather if you still feel that you need it in 10 or 30 days, then go back and get it. If it's a unique item that you will never ever find again, well do you *really, really* need it?

4. Destash
This issue is difficult for some people for emotional reasons and for others for technical reasons. I try to take a pragmatic, business-like approach to getting rid of stuff, an out with the old in with the new attitude. My children have begun to ask me to keep some things, so I include them in this decision making process, which yes makes it more work! It's ideal if you can 'destash' on a regular basis, at least once a year. Sell your unused stuff. If you can afford to give it away, that's great, but you are going to undoubtedly be needing to buy more stuff, so why not pad your budget a bit by selling valuable curriculum, toys, and sporting goods that aren't in use? Small ticket items may not be worth the trouble of reselling unless you can bundle them, such as a 'lot' of baby board books. You can do this informally through homeschooling and parenting groups online. You can list items on Ebay or through neighborhood sites like Craigslist or take them to shops that buy used children's items. It would be great if you can participate in a group yard or trunk sale.

There is an Islamic principle to not headlessly collect things. As long as you keep in mind that your intention for having all this stuff is to educate your child(ren) and make it a regular practice to unburden yourself of items you truly don't need, that should give you some relief.

* https://www.houselogic.com/organize-maintain/cleaning-decluttering/clutter-depression/

Chapter 4
OUR FAVOURITE RESOURCES

Bullet Journaling with Kids

By Karrie Chariton

While walking the school supplies aisles at my local Target, I started looking at all the pretty planners for sale. I have been feeling overwhelmed lately at the sheer amount of work I have to do and was trying to find ways to organize myself better. I wondered if a new, different planner would help. Around the same time, I had been seeing a lot on my Instagram feed and read some blog posts about something called a bullet journal. First you may ask, what is a bullet journal?

A bullet journal or "bujo" for short is a fairly new invention. It is basically a giant to-do list, planner, and diary all in one. I thought maybe this could keep me organized. I have different notebooks for blogging, homeschool resources, bill paying, miscellaneous notes from classes I have taken, menu planning, not to mention a Day-timer dated monthly planner, and a smartphone. After researching, it seemed like a bullet journal was the answer to my problems. It's a master planner that keeps track of everything all in one place! To be honest though, it seemed like it would take hours to set up a whole new system and would take too much time to learn.

After watching a few YouTube videos and familiarizing myself with the whole concept, I saw how I could easily adapt it to my needs. I was converted! I found a partially used journal I already had and set it up in less than 15 minutes. It does take longer if you are transferring/rewriting notes or lists from one place to another but this can also be done over time.

I was so enamored by this bullet journal after only one week, I started my kids on their own journals. I was in need of a planner for my new high schooler. One of her textbooks suggested using a calendar to keep track of assignments. I wanted her to be more independent and take ownership of her schoolwork. My eldest is an organizer, list maker, and already wrote daily in a journal, so I thought she would love this. For my younger two, I make a weekly assignment sheet that they cross off each subject as they complete the day's work. I thought why not make a bullet journal? I could combine it with their book list and add some other things too.

After researching online bullet journaling for kids and homeschoolers, I came across some great ideas for my family. Some homeschool families use the journal as a yearly record. I already kept a separate spreadsheet of assignments and had physical file folders of work for each child. A bullet journal could be a combination of all of this, and the best thing is it doesn't fall on me to do it. Your kids can take responsibility for writing everything down! Some other ideas I found

useful were:
- a yearly master book list with date, title, author, and page count of books read or
- a book list to follow and cross off as they read them during the year
- goals for each child
- gratitude pages
- list of state requirements that need to be fulfilled
- unit studies
- Qur'an memorization chart
- prayer tracker chart to get your children into the habit of the 5 daily prayers
- weekly/daily assignment lists
- free-form journal writing (we brainstorm different writing prompts and then write a paragraph/page/and illustrate it)
- inspirational quotes, hadiths or Quran quotes perfect for handwriting practice
- doodling is encouraged to make the journal personalized, so it becomes an art journal too!

Bullet journals can be useful even for your youngest children. Here are three ways your child can benefit:

1. Young children will gain a concrete understanding of the days of the week and months of the year. How many times are you asked, "How many days until Eid?" or "How many days until …"? Now they have a visual picture and can count themselves.

2. It gives them ownership. This is their journal and their record. You are the guide of course, but they can personalize it and also add in their drawings, lists, notes, and ideas.

3. They learn time management and organizational skills. These are invaluable skills young and old need to master. Children can learn at a young age how to use the planner by making lists and keeping track of holidays or chores. Older children can make to do lists, keep track of appointments, class assignments, tests, etc. Kids can look ahead and plan. They can see that they have a test in a week and can then plan to start studying early.

How to Make a Simple Bullet Journal:

All you need to get started is a clean notebook and a pen or pencil.

Number the pages in advance, starting at 1. You can do the whole notebook or perhaps the first 20-30 pages to get them started.

Label the very first page "Index" and save the next three pages for the index. The index acts as the table of contents for everything in your journal. Need to find something specific? Look at your index to find what page it is on. So the first line of your index will read, "Index" and write "p. 1-4". Every time you start a new page (or pages in case of a page spread), it gets indexed.

Then make p.5 as a key. You can use the symbols recommended at www.bulletjournal.com or make up your own. Just be sure to use them for consistency. An example would be "-" Task, "X" it once the task is complete, "!" for priority, "T" for test, etc. To make keying easier for younger kids, it could be color coded.

After that, you can organize the pages as you want to customize them. You may want to start with master page lists or with a month at a glance page, weekly or daily page spreads. It is totally customizable to your child's needs and preferences. You can't make a mistake. If a weekly spread isn't working for you, turn the page, and change it to one page per day or two pages per day. Use some of the ideas listed above or brainstorm your own. I have created a prayer tracker and weekly assignment tracker that will be used repeatedly so I made it in Excel to print them as needed. The kids can cut them out, glue them onto a page in their journal, and decorate if they want.

Make it fun by using different color pens, pencils, and markers, stickers, washi tape, and so on to beautify. There are plenty of ideas on Pinterest on how to make fancy numbers, banners, and page layouts. I have read that many who journal have improved their handwriting.

Your bullet journal can be as simple as you like or as fancy as you like. Once you start searching the web, there are special bullet journals for purchase that already have index pages and page numbers. The sky is the limit! These are all extras and up to you and your budget. Enjoy and get organized!

Resources and inspirations....

http://bulletjournal.com/ - the original system that started the whole thing also has a video overview

http://help.bulletjournal.com/article/30-free-starter-guide - quick reference guide translated in 15 languages

http://libertyhillhouse.com/2014/12/27/homeschool-bullet-journal

http://www.bohoberry.com/bullet-journal-101-overview/ - you can read her blog, check out her Pinterest boards, and watch videos at her Boho Berry YouTube Channel, starting with pre-planning your journal https://youtu.be/pPkEoH4vx6U

www.MariamPoppins.com documents her journaling via her blog and posts her daily journal layouts via Instagram

www.pinterest.com/theconvertlife - I have started a Bullet Journal board for inspiration and information

Typingclub.com is Mom Approved

By Karrie Chariton

Last school year I tried a keyboarding program with my children and it was awful. It started out as a novelty, but then turned into drudgery, so I finally quit forcing them to do it. I am trying again after another homeschool family praised the use of a free internet program called www.typingclub.com. What did I have to lose?

Instantly, both my children loved it. They even do it on the weekends, which has always been a forbidden time for doing schoolwork in their minds. Typing Club allows for multiple users. I created different sign ins for each child since it keeps their progress. This program tests speed and accuracy. It is flexible and allows the student to jump around and practice other letters so they won't get bored. That was one complaint my daughter had of the previous program. Typing "aaaaajjjjjssssskkkkk" was quite boring and nonsensical. She likes learning to type the letters and then practices typing real words. Typing club is very visual. There is a stats page where you can see what stars and badges you have earned, another area keeps your stats of how many words per minute you can type, accuracy, and the total time spent for each session. My son spent 40 minutes on one session, which is incredible that it held his attention for that long. Both children enjoy this stats part and use it as a little friendly competition between them. Who's fastest? Nothing like a little competition to keep things interesting.

The program starts with teaching the lowercase home row, top row, and then bottom row. They then have 14 lessons with those lower case letters to work on improving their speed before moving to upper case letters. Again, they work on speed before moving to numbers, more speed work, and then lastly symbols. By the time they are done working through the levels, they should be up to 45 words per minute, if not faster, and of course accurate. Parents and children can see their improvement through a line chart and everything is documented. As a mom to multiple children, anytime I can find a hands off curriculum for myself, I want to give it a try. One child can be at the computer doing Typing Club, while I work with another. It is a win/win for all.

Best Children's Cookbooks For Hands On Educational Fun

By Klaudia Khan

Before our children leave the nest it is good idea to train them in some basic life skills, especially cooking. There are kids who love to be in the kitchen licking bowls and getting dusty with flour, and there are those who cannot be bothered. For the enthusiastic and the uninterested there are quite a few great cookbooks to inspire learning new skills, exploring new foods and eating healthy. Because a good cookbook is more than just a collection of recipes. This is a list of my favourites:

For the absolute beginners:

• *The Tickle Fingers Toddler Cookbook* by Annabel Woolmer (Vermillion) is a one of a kind guide to cooking with the littlest ones. The recipes in the book are suitable for children aged one to four years. If you are unsure whether they could cook – well, some kids don't even eat by themselves at this age – the book is going to show you how and why you should have fun in the kitchen with your babies. All recipes for breakfast, snacks, lunch, dinner, and even pudding are toddler friendly and require no sharp knives, no stove use, and no raw meat, plus each recipe includes allergy information and parent-only preparation tasks are clearly listed.

• *Cool Kids Cook* by Jenny Chandler (Pavilion) is certainly much more than a recipe collection, it is actually a complete cookery course for budding chefs aged seven and upwards with great recipes for real food. The book aims to give kids confidence and independence, so there is a large section on safety in the kitchen, but also advice on shopping for groceries, composing flavours, and even tidying the kitchen. I also loved the fabulous facts sections explaining the science behind the cooking. Each recipe has step-by-step photographs that make them really easy to follow, and once you learn the basic version there are some interesting variations to try.

• *How to Cook in 10 Easy Lessons* by Wendy Sweetser (QED) is another great source for aspiring cooks aged seven and up. It focuses on teaching basic cooking techniques starting with using knives, through peeling, crushing, and mashing, to more advanced skills such as frying, roasting, and kneading. There is also a good selection of recipes utilising each skill with step-by-step illustrations and quick tips to make things easier.

For the reluctant chefs
• *Moomins Cookbook* by Tove Jansson and Sami Malila (Self Made Hero) is a cookbook without photos of impeccable dishes and without an ingredients index. The only pictures you get here are the illustrations from the Moomin books, some of them remotely related to the recipes, all in black and white. Some of the recipes here are very basic, like making tea or preparing sandwiches, others might require some experience in the kitchen. There are no step-by-step instructions. And yet this is one of our favourite cookbooks. My daughters, aged six and four, love it and leaf through it more frequently than through other colourful recipe books. Why? Well, we do love Moomins... and if a simple dish of boiled peas is called "Moominmamma's Special Peas" then we are going to cook them and eat them. Now, I know that not everyone is a fan of Moomins, but there are other character cookbooks that might just persuade your kitchen helpers to roll their sleeves up. You could try: Roald Dahl's Revolting Recipes, Star Wars Cookbook or even the Disney Princess Cookbook.

• If your child can't be even persuaded to open a cookbook or if you want to expand their culinary horizons try **Around The World with The Ingreedies** by Zoe Bather and Joe Sharpe (Laurence King). Ingreedies are a bunch of cartoon explorers travelling around the world in search of new taste adventures. Together with them we learn geography, history, and culture of our food, and if we feel inspired we may try some simple recipes from various cooking traditions. It's great foodie fun, even without cooking.

For the little chefs
• *The Great British Bake Off Learn to Bake* by Linda Collister is a great choice if it's baking that your child enjoys the most. There are 80 recipes for cakes, cupcakes, biscuits, breads, pudding and pastries, sweet and savoury, simple and a bit complex, for all seasons. The recipes are easy to follow with step-by-step instructions, and there are some lovely pictures as well as lots of great photos of kids playing outdoors. The design is a bit unconventional, but it does make the book look fresh and inviting.

• *Let's Cook Italian* by Anna Prandoni, *Let's Cook Spanish* by Gabriela Llamas and *Let's Cook French* by Claudine Pepin (Quarry) is a series of family cookbooks with great popular recipes to cook together. Quite a number of dishes in each of the books are too complex for children to tackle on their own, but there is advice on how to involve kids in preparation and there are great family stories and cultural background to each recipe that could spark some really interesting kitchen conversations or even inspire you to write your own family cookbook. Another great feature of these books is that each of them is bilingual: English-Italian, English-Spanish and English-French. Bon apettit, cucina di casa, por favor.

For everybody
• *Complete Children's Cookbook* (Dorling Kingsley) with more than 150 recipes for breakfast, soups, salads, snacks, main meals, desserts, and cakes this book is certainly not going to disappoint you. With this many recipes everyone will find something to their likes and the beautiful pictures of completed dishes as well as step-by-step photo instructions are really appealing. About half of the recipes in the book are for sweet dishes: desserts, cakes, and biscuits (cookies) of all kinds. The *Complete Children's Cookbook* is a good ol' traditional kind of

cookbook but, with classic dishes and some fresh ideas, there's plenty to learn from.

• *The Silver Spoon for Children* by Amanda Grant (Phaidon) is the children's edition of *The Silver Spoon* – an Italian cookbook bestseller for fifty years. It covers the classics: pizzas and pastas, as well as lighter snacks and desserts. The recipes are specially selected for children's abilities and explained in clear step-by-step instructions. Probably the best aspect of this book is its illustrations; they are funny and eye-catching while at the same time convey the instructions. Altogether a lovely book.

• *Big Meals for Little Fingers* by Virginie Aladjiji and Caroline Pellissier (Flying Eye Books) is a cookbook like no other. The recipes are prepared by French Michelin starred chef Sebastian Guenard and are equally appealing to little foodies and grown-up connoisseurs. They are simple, yet unique, and really tasty. We have tried quite a few. Even though the dishes featured in the book require adult preparation, the book itself is extremely attractive to small children because of the charming illustrations by the prolific artist Marion Billet. The recipes are divided into four seasons and then by main ingredients, making the book a great tool to teach children about seasonal produce and inspire them to try new flavours. It's one of the favourite cookbooks in our family.

• *Kids' Kitchen* by Fiona Bird (Barefoot Books) is not a book, but a set of recipe cards in a box. All the recipes here are vegetarian, which also means halal and healthy. The cards are sturdy enough to survive kitchen mess and colourful enough to attract the kids. The recipes are grouped into five colour-coded sections: Eggs'n'Beans, Fantastic Fruits, Milk'n'Dairy, Spuds'n'Grains and Vital Vegetables. My kids love to play with the cards by shuffling them and then displaying them in various ways. The colourful collage illustrations also inspire them to try the recipes.

Our Contributors

Thank you, jazakAllah khairan to all the parents who have contributed their knowledge and shared their stories to *Fitra Journal*. If you have begun homeschooling, or even parenting, you know how these tasks can absorb every minute of your day. We are truly honored that you took the time for all of us.

Asma Ali is an avid reader, writer, and dreamer who currently resides in KSA where she part-time homeschools her sons. She also writes for *Little Explorers*, an Islamic magazine for children.

Zawjah Ali writes for *Hiba* blog and magazine, *SISTERS Magazine*, the *Muslimah Network* and other Muslim media. She has done A levels and was halfway through graduation in psychology when she got married, and is now a homemaker and mother of two, alhumdulillah.

Iqra Arfeen is 17 years old, the eldest of six: five girls and one boy. She was a homeschooling student who completed her exams last year. She has many hobbies, some of which are reading, spending time with friends and family, baking, and playing PS4. She also has a passion for writing, whether it be stories or articles.

Brooke Benoit is running her own private Sudbury-like school with her seven children on the southern coast of Morocco. She is an editor for *SISTERS magazine*, the founder of *Fitra Journal*, a writing workshop facilitator and co-host of The Big Reconnect Sleepover retreats for Muslim women (and sometimes their family members).

Karrie Chariton is a homeschooling mom of three and blogger at www.theconvertlife.com. She helps converts discover the resources and support they need on their journey as Muslims. Karrie shares her experiences as a convert, which includes living in Muslim-majority countries for five years, and she also writes about being a homeschool mom in hopes of helping other Muslims who are interested in homeschooling.

Dr Gemma Elizabeth is a homeschooling mother of three from the U.K. As a passionate advocate for home education, she writes widely on the subject for various publications and speaks to mothers across the country about the benefits of homeschooling. In between the science experiments, read-alouds, and math drills, she finds time to make videos for Youtube and writes on her blog OurMuslimHomeschool.com.

Khalida Haque is a qualified and experienced counselling psychotherapist who has a private practice, is a clinical supervisor, group facilitator, freelance writer, and counselling services manager, as well as founder and managing director of Khair (www.khair-therapeutic.com). She is a mother of three with an on-off homeschooling tendency, having been guided by her and her children's needs.

Reyhana Ismail is a UK-based graphic designer who specializes in print design, with a primary focus on books and magazines. She is the Design Director of *SISTERS magazine* and has her own freelance design firm, Rey of Light. Reyhana enjoys baking, art, and travelling with her two kids, and is also a keen swimmer.

Klaudia Khan is a Muslim mum and writer living in Yorkshire, UK. She has three homeschooled daughters and loves to learn, create, and play with them.

Umm Yusuf Aisha Lbhalla is a homeschooling mom of two lively boys aged eleven and five. They enjoy making movies for their YouTube channel *The Islamic Adventures of Yusuf and Hasan* and their hobbies include all things Lego and Minecraft. In Aisha's spare time, she is a small business owner of a home care agency which provides assistance with activities of daily living to the elderly and disabled in their homes. She chairs the Muslim Women's Council whose primary goal is to share a correct understanding of Islam and Muslims particularly regarding Muslim women to the public. She also serves as a Commissioner on the Metro Human Relations Commission whose task is to protect and promote the personal dignity, peace, safety, security, health, and general welfare of all people in her city.

Zakiya Mahomed-Kalla is an education enthusiast and an aspiring linguist. She tutors Economics for the University of South Africa, and Arabic for the love of it. See more of her writing at zakiyamahomed.com

Angeliqua Rahhali is an artist, home-educator, counselor, cultural anthropologist, writer, and explorer. She loves learning and can often be found researching everything, from how things are made and where they come from, to the next destination she wants to learn about and culture to embrace. She loves reading, playing brain games, and experimenting with fusions of flavors in her kitchen.

Karrie Marie, Virtual Assistant
@ karriemarie.com

Supporting women entrepreneurs by building their online presence and tackling their to-do lists so they can focus on their business growth.

Education is the key...

Help nurture your child's Islamic education!

Free Delivery Order over £40

0754 106 1522
info@almuttaqun.com

Please visit us at:
www.almuttaqun.com

10% Off when you like & share us at:
/almuttaqunshop
@almuttaqun_shop
al_muttaqun_shop

Playful books for faithful children
ANEESA Books

- Muslim Rhymes and Lullabies
- Hector Hectricity and the Missing Socks
- Peace and Thanks on the Farm (colouring book and picture book)
- and more

www.aneesabooks.com

1001 FREE Resources
for
Muslim Homeschoolers

Get your **Free e-Book** today!

OurMuslimHOMESCHOOL.COM

BROOKE BENOIT
Homeschool Strategist

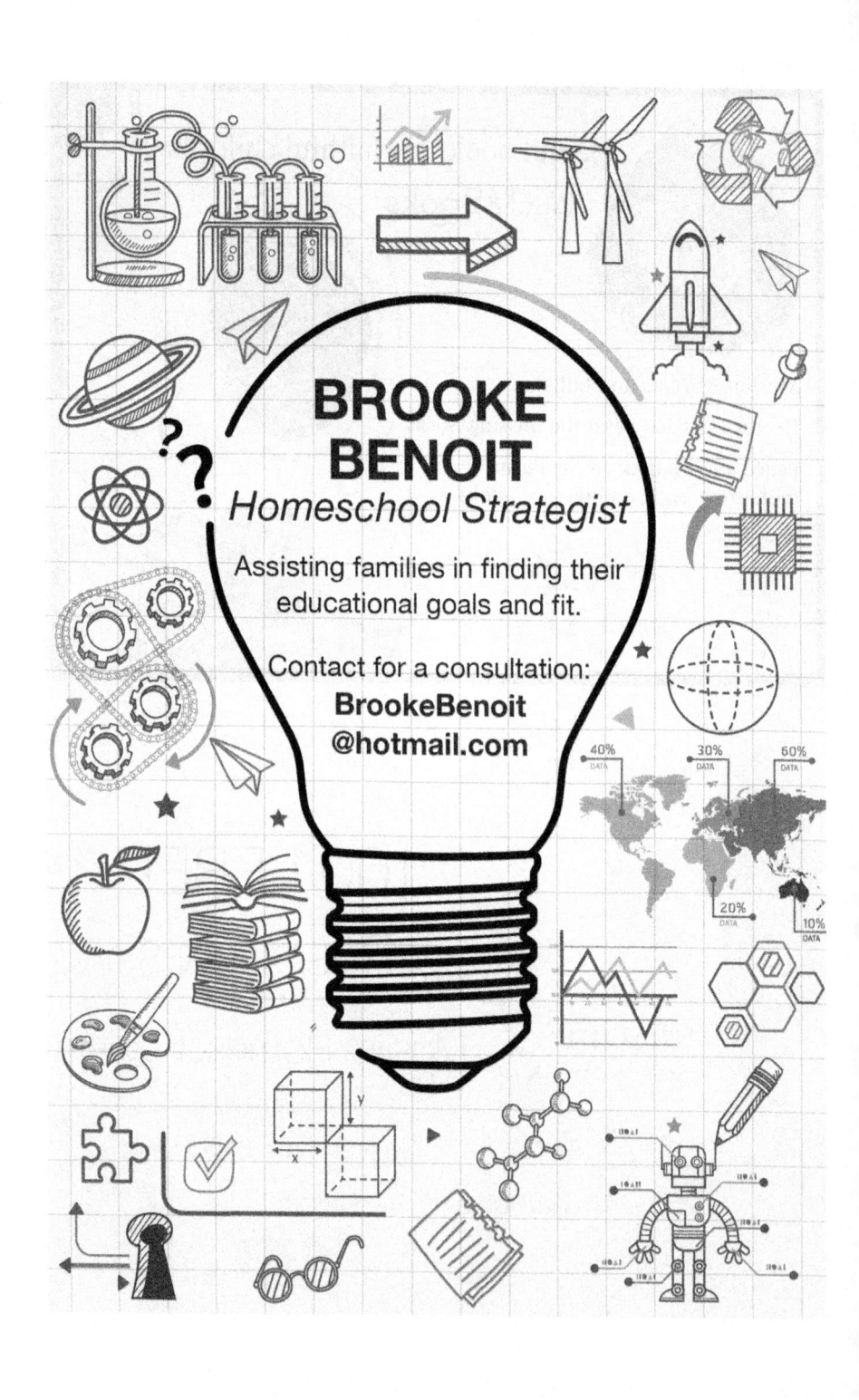

Assisting families in finding their educational goals and fit.

Contact for a consultation:
BrookeBenoit@hotmail.com

Online Homeschooling Course

Islamic Self Help invites you to our online course for parents who homeschool.

This course covers the ins and outs of homeschooling, to make homeschooling easier for you.

We are offering a special 50% discount to readers of the *Fitra Journal*.

Use the following link to claim your discount:
http://bit.ly/2pgT7Pb

ISLAMIC SELF HELP
by Shaykh Ismail Kamdar